Expertise

A Technical Guide to Ceramics

Expertise
A Technical Guide to Ceramics

CHARLOTTE F. SPEIGHT

JOHN TOKI
California College of the Arts

McGraw Hill

Boston   Burr Ridge, IL   Dubuque, IA   Madison, WI   New York   San Francisco   St. Louis
Bangkok   Bogotá   Caracas   Kuala Lumpur   Lisbon   London   Madrid   Mexico City
Milan   Montreal   New Delhi   Santiago   Seoul   Singapore   Sydney   Taipei   Toronto

Higher Education

EXPERTISE: A TECHNICAL GUIDE TO CERAMICS

Published by McGraw-Hill, an imprint of The McGraw-Hill Companies, Inc. 1221 Avenue of the Americas, New York, NY 10020. Copyright © 2004 by the McGraw-Hill Companies, Inc. All rights reserved. No part of this publication may be reproduced or distributed in any form or by any means, or stored in a database or retrieval system, without the prior written permission of The McGraw-Hill Companies, Inc., including but not limited to, in any network or other electronic storage or transmission, or broadcast for distance learning.

Some ancillaries, including electronic and print components, may not be available to customers outside the United States.

This book is printed on acid-free paper.

1 2 3 4 5 6 7 8 9 0 QPD/QPD 0 9 8 7 6 5 4 3

ISBN: 0-07-294249-5

Publisher: Chris Freitag
Sponsoring editor: Joe Hanson
Development editor: Carolyn Smith
Marketing manager: Lisa Berry
Production editor: Jennifer Chambliss
Production supervisor: Richard De Vitto
Design manager: Cassandra Chu
Compositor: Thompson Type
Typeface: 10/12 Melior
Printer: Quebecor World Dubuque

Library of Congress Cataloging In-Publication Data

Speight, Charlotte F., 1919–
    Expertise : a technical guide to ceramics / Charlotte F. Speight, John Toki.
        p. cm.
    Includes bibliographical references.
    ISBN 0-07-294249-5
        1. Pottery craft. I. Toki, John. II. Title.

TT920.S683 2003
738--dc21

                                                                        2003053971

www.mhhe.com

The information in *Expertise* is designed to supplement the information in the main text, *Hands in Clay*. It includes a series of clay and glaze tests that you can follow in progression using the accompanying charts. If you work through the clay and glaze tests in Chapter 1A, you will develop a basic understanding of both the composition and the qualities of different clay bodies and glazes. Chapter 2 provides useful information for programming your kiln and firing your tests and ware. If you want to go deeper into testing and glaze calculation, Chapter 3 provides an example of changing the flux in a glaze and follows a potter calculating, testing, and modifying a high-fire glaze. It also includes charts of chemical information you will need. Chapter 4 lists various types of plaster formulas and their applications, as well as solutions to typical problems one experiences when making plaster molds and slip-casting. It also covers the considerations one makes when installing ceramic pieces on walls or outdoors. Chapter 5 lists sources of health and safety information and suppliers of equipment and materials.

CONTENTS

1A

Clays and Glazes Formulated for Testing

The following recipes were formulated for *Hands in Clay* to provide a learning experience for mixing and testing clay bodies and glazes. The clay recipes will produce clay bodies with various qualities and firing temperatures, while the glaze recipes will give you practice in changing the color of a base glaze. Testing is only a means to extend your creativity in clay. What makes a successful ceramic technician and artist? He or she must maintain a bright spirit, solid determination, and hope for a dash of luck!

CLAY BODIES FOR TESTING

Although the clay body tests were fired at cone 05, cone 5, and cone 10, allowing for a wide range of firing temperatures, the actual range of the cones and temperatures for these tests is less rigid than the charts imply. For example, the low-fire white clay can be fired as low as cone 010 and as high as cone 1, whereas the cone 5 porcelain develops a richer sheen when fired at cone 7 or even as high as cone 10. Changes in firing temperatures will affect the shrinkage and color of the clay, and changes in components will affect the workability of the body. While you are developing your own clay bodies through tests, it is wise to be flexible about material substitutes, temperatures, and kiln atmospheres. Each of these factors will subtly affect the outcome of your tests, adding to the excitement as you proceed. Do not be discouraged from mixing clays or glazes if the names of the materials listed in the following recipes are not the same as those in your area. For example, the names of fire clays, ball clays, and feldspars will vary depending on where you live. You will just have to test the substitutes thoroughly.

Hands in Clay Cone 05, 5, and 10 White Clay Bodies   (CL1, CL2, CL3, CL4)

Components	Percentage		
	Cone 05 (CL1)	Cone 5 (CL2)	Cone 10 (CL3, CL4)
Kentucky ball clay (OM4)	50.0	21.0	20.0
Kaolin (Georgia)		27.0	28.0
Fire clay (Lincoln)			
Feldspar (Custer)			25.0
Feldspar (nepheline syenite)		25.0	
Silica 200 mesh (flint)		25.0	25.0
Talc	50.0		
Macaloid		2.0	2.0

Notes:
White base clay bodies in oxidation (CL1 to CL3):
   Cone 05—smooth, warm-white body (CL1)
   Cone 5—smooth, slightly off-white (CL2)
   Cone 10—smooth, slightly off-white (CL3)
White base clay bodies in reduction:
   Cone 10—smooth, light gray (CL4)

Components of Blended Clay Bodies

BALL CLAY   Ball clay has highly plastic qualities, and for that reason it is used in both low-fire and high-fire clay bodies that require plasticity—for example, those to be thrown on the wheel. It is also used in low-fire slip for casting bodies.

FIRE CLAY   Maturing at a high temperature and readily available and inexpensive, fire clay is used in stoneware bodies to provide silica and alumina, refractory materials, and to increase the heat-resistant quality of the clay. Fire clays are relatively plastic.

TALC   Talc is a magnesium-bearing rock that sometimes contains impurities of iron and alumina as well as alkalies and lime. Because of its magnesium content, it is used as a flux for low-fire clays and casting slips.

FELDSPARS   Feldspathic rocks are among the most common rocks in the earth's crust, and the feldspars used in ceramics come from those rocks as they are broken down by geologic forces. Feldspars contain alumina, silica, and, depending on the composition of the particular feldspar, varying amounts of sodium, potassium, or calcium. Feldspars are heat resistant and are used as a principal flux in stoneware clays, because stoneware is heated to temperatures high enough to melt the feldspar (above 2192°F/1200°C). Since feldspars mined in different places vary in composition, it is important to know the chemical formula of the feldspar you use.

Clay Bodies Formulated for Use in Color and Glaze Tests

The following clay bodies were mixed in 300-g batches. The clays were first blended dry; then they were mixed with water into a slip. For the smooth clay bodies, the water content was about 20% of the batch, while the bodies with 20% grog required roughly 13–15% water content per batch. The slip was poured onto a plaster bat and left 5 to 10 minutes or until enough moisture had been absorbed to bring the clay to the right consistency for wedging. The base recipes for these clay bodies were formulated to total 100%. Coloring oxides and stains were added to the base clay in varying percentages. The letters and numbers in parentheses refer to the test tiles in *Hands in Clay*, Figure 10-11. Be sure to follow the precautions given in Chapter 10 for handling dry clay when you mix these clay bodies.

Substitutions for the materials and chemicals listed in the recipes will cause changes in the color, texture, and firing range of the clays. If you substitute, you will need to carry out additional tests. Some possible substitutes include:

- *Kaolin:* EPK or Grolleg or other kaolin may be substituted for Georgia.
- *Feldspar:* Locally available feldspars such as Unispar 50, G-200, or Kona F-4 may be substituted for Custer, a potash feldspar.
- *Fire clay:* Fire clays such as IMCO#400 or #800, Cedar Heights, Goldart, Pine Lake, Hawthorne Bond, or Missouri may be substituted for Lincoln.

- *Ball clay:* Bandy, CP-7, Copper Light, Taylor, Champion and Challenger, Black Charm, Jackson.
- *Macaloid:* Assists in giving plasticity to some clays; it may be eliminated for test purposes, or vee gum or bentonite can be substituted.
- *Any red earthenware,* such as C-Red, Newman, Laterite, Redart, Kreth Red, or Cedar Heights Redart terra-cotta, can be substituted for the Red Horse clay.
- *Stains:* Other pink or yellow (praseodymium) glaze or body stains may be substituted, as can other color stains. Be aware of the maximum cone or temperature range of whatever stain you substitute, because some colors fade at high temperatures (D320 pink and #6440 tin-

vanadium yellow are both high-temperature stains).

Coloring Clay Bodies with Natural Clays (CL5 to CL8)

To make subtle changes in the color of a clay body, you may simply wedge two colors of clay together to create a lighter or darker shade. However, the following clays for testing were mixed dry, and then water was added to make a slip that was poured onto a plaster bat to absorb the water and stiffen the clay. (See the general instructions for mixing clay bodies in *Hands in Clay,* Chapter 10.)

Components	Percentage		
	Cone 05 (CL5)	Cone 5 (CL6)	Cone 10 (CL7)
Kentucky ball clay (OM4)	30.0		35.0
Earthenware (Red Horse)*	50.0	50.0	
Fire clay (Lincoln)		50.0	65.0
Talc	20.0		

*For test purposes, Red Horse clay can be substituted with C-Red, Kreth Red, Redart, or any red earthenware clay.

Notes:
Coloring white clay bodies with natural clays:
    Cone 05—warm light red, smooth (would burnish well) (CL5)
    Cone 5—rust-red, slightly grainy (CL6)
    Cone 10 oxidation—gray-buff, smooth (CL7)
    Cone 10 reduction—warm brown, smooth (CL8)

Texturing Clay Bodies with Grog/Fillers/Tempers (CL9 to CL12)

To give differing textures to clay bodies, you can introduce various types of grog or filler in place of the buff grog (30–70 mesh) or the **molochite.** You can also blend the texturing materials in combinations, adding even greater tooth and openness to the clay body. For example, for a sculpture body use half sand, half grog, or a variety of mesh sizes of sand, grog and pearlite in combination.

Components	Percentage			
	Cone 05 (CL9)	Cone 5 (CL10)	Cone 10(A) (CL11)	Cone 10(B) (CL12)
Kentucky ball clay (OM4)	40.0	50.0	28.0	28.0
Kaolin (Georgia)				
Fire clay (Lincoln)		30.0	52.0	52.0
Feldspar (Custer)				
Silica 200 mesh (flint)				
Talc	40.0			
Macaloid*				
Grog (buff 30–70 mesh)*	20.0	20.0	20.0	20.0
Molochite (porcelain grog)				

*Can be substituted with the following materials:

Silica sand	(30–90 mesh)	5–10% (Sand in some clay bodies fired to around cone 10 may form a gritty surface.)
Ione grain	(30–150 mesh)	5–20% (Ione grain is no longer available. For test purposes substitute with local grogs from your region.)
Red grog	(9–30 mesh)	5–20%
Pearlite	(fine or coarse)	1–5%

Notes:
Texturing clay bodies with grog/tempers:
   Cone 05—white, slightly rough surface (CL9)
   Cone 5—off-white, rough surface (CL10)
   Cone 10(A) oxidation—gray-buff, slightly rough surface (CL11)
   Cone 10(B) reduction—warm brown, lighter speckles, rough surface (CL12)

Cone 10 White Stoneware Clay Body* (WS1 Oxidation, WS2 Reduction)

Components	Percentage
Kentucky ball clay (OM4)	25.0
Silica 200 mesh (flint)	20.0
Kaolin (Georgia)	20.0
Feldspar (Custer)	20.0
Macaloid	2.0
Molochite	13.0

*A textured stoneware body for general use.

Shrinkage Test

Since clay bodies have different rates of shrinkage, when you formulate a clay body it is important to test it for shrinkage on drying and after firing. For example, the white 05 clay used in these tests shrank about 5% from wet to dry and about 6% from dry to fired state. One way to measure the amount of shrinkage of a clay is to cast a block of plaster, carve lines into it 1 in. (25.4 mm) apart, and number the lines from 1 to 10. To make a clay test tile, simply press a slab of clay onto the block to imprint the pattern of lines and numbers in the clay, then dry and fire the slab. You can then measure how much the clay shrinks after drying and firing by comparing its measurement before and after with this plaster ruler. Or you can use a commercial **shrink ruler.**

Casting Slip

Hands in Clay Cone 05 Low-Fire White Casting Slip (SL1)
Batch Formula for 128 Fluid oz. (1 gal. [3.875 l])

Components	Amount	Percentage
Kentucky ball clay (OM4)	2,027.25 g	50.0
Talc	2,027.25 g	50.0
		100% total

Additives:		
Soda ash	4.46 g	.11
Sodium silicate (N)	18.65 g (fluid wt.)	.46
Water	1,900.60 g (67 fluid oz.)	46.69 g (1.65 fluid oz.) water per 100-g batch

Notes:
Weigh the deflocculants sodium silicate and soda ash on a gram scale and mix with water. Add talc and ball clay and mix for 30 minutes, then screen the slip through a 40- to 60-mesh sieve. Accurate sequence, measurement, and mixing time are crucial to suspension and fluidity, and screening is essential for smoothness. Be sure to follow the given sequence in mixing the components, the water, and the sodium silicate. Immediately before casting, slip should be mixed again for 1 to 2 minutes. See Chapter 13 in *Hands in Clay* for pouring directions.

Hands in Clay Cones 5–7 White Porcelain Casting Slip (Electric Kiln) (SL2)
Batch Formula for 128 Fluid oz. (1 gal. [3.875 l])

Components	Amount	Percentage
Kaolin (Georgia)	1,380.0 g	25.0
Feldspar (Custer)	552.0 g	10.0
Feldspar (Nepheline syenite)	1,656.0 g	30.0
Silica 325 mesh (flint)	552.0 g	10.0
Kentucky ball clay (OM4)	1,380.0 g	25.0
		100% total

Additives:		
Soda ash	5.52 g	.10
Sodium silicate (N)	22.08 g (fluid wt.)	.40
Darvan #7	13.80 g (fluid wt.)	.25
Water	1,564.92 g (55.20 fluid oz.)	55.60 g (2.0 fluid oz.) water per 100-g batch

Notes:
Follow the same measuring and mixing directions as for the cone 05 slip. For casting an object with fine detail, it is a good idea to put the slip through a ball mill. You may also want to use up to an 80-mesh sieve to screen the slip. In that case, you probably will have to push the slip through with a flexible spatula. One way to check the amount of water needed in the casting slips is to measure out 1 pint (.48 l) of slip and weigh it. If it weighs less than 26–28.5 oz. (735.8–806.6 g) for low-fire slip, or less than 28.5–32 oz. (806.6–905.6 g) for high-fire slip, your mixture has too much water. This could cause settling.

Hands in Clay Cones 10–11 White Porcelain Casting Slip (for Gas or Electric Kiln) (SL3)
Batch formula for 128 Fluid oz. (1 gal. [3.875 l])

Components	Amount	Percentage
Kaolin (Grolleg)	1,951.20 g	40.0
Feldspar (Custer)	1,219.50 g	25.0
Silica 325 mesh (flint)	975.60 g	20.0
Kentucky ball clay (OM4)	731.70 g	15.0
		100% total

Additives	Amount	Percentage
Soda ash	6.09 g	.125
Sodium silicate (N)	19.51 g (fluid wt.)	.40
Darvan #7	19.51 g (fluid wt.)	.40
Water	1,936.0 g (68.29 fluid oz.)	39.62 g (1.40 fluid oz.) water per 100-g batch

Notes:
Fired in oxidation, this is a white slip; in reduction it will be gray. Follow the same measuring and mixing directions as for the cone 05 slip. For casting an object with fine detail, it is a good idea to put the slip through a ball mill. You may also want to use up to an 80-mesh sieve to screen the slip. In that case, you probably will have to push the slip through with a flexible spatula.

Egyptian Paste

Cone 015 White Egyptian Paste* (EP1-4)

Components	Percentage
Nepheline syenite	25.0
Frit 3134	15.0
Silica 200 mesh (flint)	20.0
Silica sand 70 mesh	8.0
Kentucky ball clay (OM4)	24.0
Soda ash	3.0
Borax (powder)	3.0
Macaloid	2.0
	100% total

*The components of this clay body form an integral glaze on its surface as it is fired. (See Chapter 2 in *Hands in Clay* for historical information on Egyptian paste.)

Notes:
Mix the dry components, then add enough water to form a stiff paste. Shape it into whatever small object you wish, then dry it slowly until soluble salts form on the surface. Fire it at cone 015. Once you mix the base white body, you can experiment with a variety of stains and oxides for coloring. The following percentages will give you a starting point for your testing.

Colorants:

Turquoise: Copper carbonate	2.50%	(EP2)
Blue: Cobalt carbonate	.75%	(EP3)
Soft lavender: D320 pink stain	3.00%	(EP4)
Cobalt carbonate	.15%	

Speckling:
Granular ilmenite: forms tiny black specks
Silicon carbide (36 grit): forms prominent black specks

COLORING CLAY BODIES WITH OXIDES AND STAINS (CS1 TO CS6)

Dry stains can be mixed directly into the dry clay. In the following tests of cone 05, cone 5, and cone 10 clay in oxidation firing, the same percentages of stain were used, so only one chart is given below with notes on the colors achieved in each clay.

Stains and Oxides Added to *Hands in Clay* Cones 05, 5, and 10 White Clay Bodies

Colorants	Percentage					
	Blue (CS1)	Medium Brown (CS2)	Green (CS3)	Pink (CS4)	Yellow (CS5)	Dark Brown (CS6)
Cobalt oxide	3.0					1.0
Iron oxide (red)		5.0				4.0
Chromium oxide			3.0			2.0
Manganese oxide						3.0
D320 Pink stain				5.0		
#6440 Tin-vanadium yellow					5.0	

Notes:
Coloring code 05 white clay body with stains and oxides (oxidation) (CS1 to CS6):
  Blue—a light, rather watery blue (CS1)
  Red-brown—a light reddish brown, the color of flower pots (S2)
  Green—pale leaf green, no blue tones (CS3)
  Pink—very pale pink, almost off-white (CS4)
  Yellow—pale, beige-yellow (CS5)
  Brown—more gray than brown (CS6). On this clay, the low-fire clear glaze (G1 formula on page 9) has a milky appearance.

If you like a matt finish, fire the test without a glaze; if you want to deepen and intensify the color and add a glossy finish, apply a clear glaze.
Coloring cone 5 white clay body with stains and oxides (oxidation) (CS1 to CS6):
  Blue—rich deep blue with very slight purple tinge (CS1)
  Medium brown—warm brown (CS2)
  Green—dark leaf green (CS3)
  Pink—light pink, flesh color (CS4)
  Yellow—earthtone yellow; not clear lemon yellow (CS5)
  Dark brown—rich chocolate brown (CS6)

Applying the clear glaze over these clays does not intensify the color but adds a glossy surface.
Coloring cone 10 white clay body with stains and oxides (oxidation) (CS1 to CS6):
  Blue—very dark blue, slightly purplish tone (CS1)
  Medium brown—cold gray/brown (CS2)
  Green—yellow green (CS3)
  Pink—paler than cone 5 pink (CS4)
  Yellow—slightly yellower than cone 5 yellow (CS5)
  Dark brown—rich chocolate brown (CS6)

GUM SOLUTION FOR TRANSPARENT UNDERGLAZE STAIN OR OXIDES USED ON WHITE CLAY BODY

If you would like to make your own transparent water-based underglazes, you can mix oxides and ceramic stains using a solution of CMC gum in water in the following formula:

Basic Stain Solution

Water	CMC Gum
1 gal. (3.875 l)	130.66 g
or	
1 pint (.48 l)	16.33 g

SURFACE COLORS/ UNDERGLAZES, STAINS

Colorants (Stains and Oxides) for Use on White Clay Body

Colorant	Solution	Color: Cone 05	Color: Cone 5	Color: Cone 10
5 g Cobalt	3 oz. (91 ml)	Matt gray blue (S1)	Dark blue, slight gloss (S5)	Dark blue, slight gloss (S9)
5 g Yellow stain	3 oz. (91 ml)	Bright yellow (S3)	Pale yellow (S7)	Pale yellow (S11)
8 g Iron	3 oz. (91 ml)	Matt red-brown (S4)	Dark matt brown (S8)	Dark matt brown (S12)
5 g Chromium	3 oz. (91 ml)	Matt leaf green (S2)	Dark leaf green (S6)	Dark leaf green (S10)

You may brush, spray, or paint on the underglaze. Apply it thinly in one coat; otherwise, any glaze you use over the underglaze may crawl. The test underglazes applied with this solution were fired from cone 05 up to cone 10 in oxidation. The oxides and stains tested held their colors at these cones. You will need to make more tests to see which proportion of coloring agents will work best for you, depending on your clay and the temperature at which you fire the tests. With a coat of transparent glaze over the underglaze, the colors are generally brighter (ST1 to ST12). If you plan to keep the solution for later use, you may add a few drops of formaldehyde, but because formaldehyde can produce allergic reactions, we recommend that you mix only enough solution for immediate use.

Water Ratio

You must control the amount of water you add to the glaze materials because the proportion of water affects glaze-material suspension as well as application properties. The percentages in the following chart indicate the water-to-glaze ratio for the glaze test formulas in this appendix. Use the chart only as a guide when formulating your own test glazes. In our testing, the glazes were applied with two to three brushed-on applications. For dipping or pouring, more water would be needed. The varying porosity of bisque ware affects the water ratio. For example, Larry Murphy's cone 10 glaze (see p. 9) needs 3.4 oz. (102.91 ml) of water per 100 g of glaze for dipping. For brushing, two coats will usually suffice; for dipping, it takes one to two dips.

Once you have established the water content for a glaze through testing, if settling occurs, try reducing the amount of water and refer to the glaze-suspension chart in Chapter 1B. Start by adding .5–2% of bentonite or macaloid. Purified bentonite was used for the tests in this chapter. The addition of gums, which will thicken a glaze, may necessitate increased amounts of water.

Water Proportions for *Hands in Clay* Glazes

Glaze	Per 100 g of Glaze Material	Per 100 g of Glaze and Colorant
Hands in Clay Cone 05	2.5 oz. (75.67 ml)	2.5 oz. (75.67 ml)
Hands in Clay Cone 5	2.5 oz. (75.67 ml)	3.0 oz. (90.81 ml)
Larry Murphy's Cone 10	3.4 oz. (102.91 ml)	4.0 oz. (121.08 ml)

GLAZES FORMULATED FOR TESTING

The following glazes were tested on the white base clay body. Since a glaze consists of a combination of chemicals that fuse and adhere to a clay body under proper application and firing, both the clay body and the firing are equally important in developing successful glazes, and the two must work in a symbiotic relationship. The glazes in this section were formulated to be used on the clays that you have already tested. The cone 05 glaze fits the cone 05 clay, the cone 5 glaze fits the cone 5 clay, and the cone 10 glaze fits the white cone 10 clay.

How you apply the glaze and the type of kiln and atmosphere in which you fire it will also affect the final result. Make notes as you test so that you can make changes based on what happened in your tests. Devise a system of displaying or storing your test tiles so that they are easily available for reference. Our notes following the clay and glaze recipes describe the appearance of the test tiles after firing in a test kiln. Your tests may differ from these descriptions, and the colors or textures as they appear on these small test tiles may also look quite different on a piece of sculpture or a pot.

Glaze Recipes to Mix and Test

Hands in Clay Cone 05 Glaze Recipe (for Testing Only)

Components	Percentage							
	Clear Base (G1)	White (G2)	Blue (G3)	Brown (G4)	Green (G5)	Black (G6)	Pink (G7)	Yellow (G8)
Frit 3195 (3811) (F434)	88.0	88.0	88.0	88.0	88.0	88.0	88.0	88.0
Kaolin (Georgia)	10.0	10.0	10.0	10.0	10.0	10.0	10.0	10.0
Bentonite	2.0	2.0	2.0	2.0	2.0	2.0	2.0	2.0

Added Colorants	Percentage							
	Clear Base (G1)	White (G2)	Blue (G3)	Brown (G4)	Green (G5)	Black (G6)	Pink (G7)	Yellow (G8)
Tin oxide		12.0						
Cobalt oxide			2.0			2.0		
Iron oxide (red)				6.0		4.0		
Chromium oxide					6.0	2.5		
D320 Pink stain							7.0	
#6440 Tin-vanadium yellow								7.0

Notes:
Cone 05 tests fired in a small test kiln in oxidation:
  Clear—good clear glaze, no crackle; pencil shows (G1)
  White—glossy, almost opaque; black underglaze pencil shows through slightly (G2)
  Blue—deep blue with attractive mottling; covers pencil (G3)
  Brown—rich, opaque dark brown with golden brown areas; covers pencil (G4)
  Green—opaque shiny green; completely covers clay surface and underglaze pencil (G5)
  Black—brownish-black, slight pinholing; covers pencil (G6)
  Pink—pale pink; underglaze pencil runs but shows clearly (G7)
  Yellow—glossy yellow, more opaque than the pink; underglaze pencil shows somewhat (G8)

Hands in Clay **Cone 5 Glaze Recipe (for Testing Only)**

Components	Percentage								
	Clear Base (G9)	White (G10)	Blue (G11)	Brown (G12)	Green (G13)	Black (G14)	Pink #1 (G15A)	Pink #2 (G15B)	Yellow (G16)
Calcium carbonate (whiting)	3.0	3.0	3.0	3.0	3.0	3.0	3.0	3.0	3.0
Kaolin (Georgia)	13.0	13.0	13.0	13.0	13.0	13.0	13.0	13.0	13.0
Gerstley borate*	27.0	27.0	27.0	27.0	27.0	27.0	27.0	27.0	27.0
Nepheline syenite	45.0	45.0	45.0	45.0	45.0	45.0	45.0	45.0	45.0
PV (plastic vitrox) clay	10.0	10.0	10.0	10.0	10.0	10.0	10.0	10.0	10.0
Bentonite (purified)	2.0	2.0	2.0	2.0	2.0	2.0	2.0	2.0	2.0

Added Colorants	Percentage								
	Clear Base (G9)	White (G10)	Blue (G11)	Brown (G12)	Green (G13)	Black (G14)	Pink #1 (G15A)	Pink #2 (G15B)	Yellow (G16)
Tin oxide		12.0							
Cobalt oxide			2.0			2.0			
Iron oxide (red)				6.0		4.0			
Chromium oxide					6.0	2.5			
D320 Pink stain #1 test[†]							7.0		
F444 Pink stain #2 test[†]								7.0	
#6440 Tin-vanadium yellow									7.0

Substitutes: Leslie Ceramics Akiko Borate, Laguna Clay Co. Borate. Check with your local supplier for other substitutes.

[†]This test was run first with the Pink stain D320 in the same proportion as in the cone 05 glaze. Since no pink color showed, a new test was run with Pink stain F444 substituted, which produced a true pink at cone 5. This shows that a stain that gives true color at one cone may not hold color in another cone range. For this reason, it is important to run tests at a number of temperature ranges, using other colors of stains to see which colors hold true.

Notes:
Cone 5 glaze tests fired in a small test kiln in oxidation:
   Clear—smooth, clear, with some crackling; pencil shows (G9)
   White—semiopaque white; pencil shows slightly (G10)
   Blue—rich, smooth, and glossy dark blue; pencil covered (G11)
   Light brown—translucent golden brown; some crackle; underglaze pencil shows (G12)
   Green—shiny green, slightly darker than in cone 05 firing; covers body and pencil completely (G13)
   Black—shiny, almost a true black with only slight brown tone; covers pencil (G14)
   Pink #1—no pink color using stain D320; milky white matt; pencil shows through, blurry (G15A)
   Pink #2—stain F444 gave a true pink at this cone (G15B)
   Yellow—runny and slightly more transparent than in cone 05; pencil blurred, but shows more (G16)

Larry Murphy's (*Hands in Clay*) Cone 10 Matt Glaze Recipe*

Components				Percentage				
	Matt Base (G17)	White (G18)	Blue (G19)	Brown (G20)	Green (G21)	Black (G22)	Pink (G23)	Yellow (G24)
Kaolin (Georgia)	28.0	28.0	28.0	28.0	28.0	28.0	28.0	28.0
Silica 325 mesh (flint)	13.0	13.0	13.0	13.0	13.0	13.0	13.0	13.0
Feldspar (Custer)	35.0	35.0	35.0	35.0	35.0	35.0	35.0	35.0
Calcium carbonate (whiting)	24.0	24.0	24.0	24.0	24.0	24.0	24.0	24.0

Added Colorants				Percentage				
	Matt Base (G17)	White (G18)	Blue (G19)	Brown (G20)	Green (G21)	Black (G22)	Pink (G23)	Yellow (G24)
Tin oxide		12.0†						
Cobalt oxide			2.0			2.0		
Iron oxide				6.0		4.0		
Chrome oxide					6.0	2.5		
D320 Pink							7.0	
#6440 Tin-vanadium yellow								7.0

*Very slightly changed from the proportions given for this glaze in Chapter 3A.) (G17 to G32)

†Varying quantities of tin oxide may affect glaze smoothness and will affect opacity.

Notes:
Cone 10 glaze tests fired in small test kiln in oxidation:
  Murphy formulated this to be a cone 10 matt. The surface is smooth and pleasantly matt, the colors more subtle as a result. The glaze was applied on the *Hands in Clay* cone 10 white test clay (CL3, CL4 on page 2) rather than on Murphy's stoneware clay because the white clay provided a better background for testing color.

  Matt—semiopaque (G17)
  White—completely opaque (G18)
  Blue—handsome, matt blue, softer color than when shiny (G19)
  Brown—still golden brown tinge, but darker than at cone 5; slightly rough surface (G20)
  Green—deep green (G21)
  Black—truer black than either of the other glazes (G22)
  Pink—the brightest pink of all! Semiopaque with the underglaze pencil fuzzy but quite clear (G23)
  Yellow—soft, almost golden yellow; pencil shows (G24)

Cone 10 glaze tests fired in gas kiln in reduction:
  Matt base—semimatt white; underglaze pencil shows (G25)
  White—yellowish pale beige (G26)
  Blue—deep blue, matt, slightly mottled (G27)
  Brown—yellowish brown (G28)
  Green—semimatt green (G29)
  Black—semimatt black (G30)
  Pink—pale pink; underglaze pencil shows (G31)
  Yellow—turned gray with some white speckles, which came from the clay (G32)

Line Blend Testing

After testing any combination of *Hands in Clay* glazes from G1 to G24, you can continue developing glazes by line blend testing. If you take 90% (by volume) of the *Hands in Clay* cone 05 clear base glaze (G1) and blend it with 10% of (G3) blue, you will achieve a light-blue transparent glaze. If you continue the process and blend 80% of the clear with 20% of the blue, you will have a slightly darker blue transparent glaze and so on. By continuing in this manner and changing percentages of the glazes, you will end up with nine different shades of blue.

You can take this process a step further by blending one of these glazes with another glaze to develop yet another color. For example, to make a blue-green transparent glaze, blend one of your light-blue transparent glazes with a green glaze such as G5.

Although used primarily for achieving color variations in glazes, line blend testing can also be used to test changes in ingredients in order to affect any glaze's maturing point. For example, to lower the maturing of a high-fire glaze such as *Hands in Clay* cone 10 matt glaze, G17, you could perform a line blend test by blending 90% of G17 with 10%

of *Hands in Clay* cone 5 clear base, G9. Then continue this process by blending 80% of the high-fire glaze G17 with 20% of the cone 5 clear, G9. As you continue increasing the proportion of the cone 5 glaze to the high-fire glaze, you will gradually lower its maturing point. The surface color and texture of the glazes will also be affected: One glaze will be matt and the other a gloss glaze.

Using this method of testing, you will also be able to explore the wide ranges of glazes between cone 05 (1915°F/1046°C) and cone 10 (2377°F/1303°C). You can best understand this process by following through a line blend test. The test shown in the following table uses two *Hands in Clay* glazes, G1 Clear and G3 Blue.

Sample Line Blend Test

Base Glaze Clear G1	100%	Base Glaze Blue G3	100%
Test 1	90%	Test 1	10%
Test 2	80%	Test 2	20%
Test 3	70%	Test 3	30%
Test 4	60%	Test 4	40%
Test 5	50%	Test 5	50%
Test 6	40%	Test 6	60%
Test 7	30%	Test 7	70%
Test 8	20%	Test 8	80%
Test 9	10%	Test 9	90%

Note:
If necessary, the percentages shown in the chart can be changed to grams, pounds, ounces, spoonfuls, tablespoons, cups, liters, quarts, gallons, or any other measure you wish to use. For example, 90% can equal 9 grams, 9 ounces, 9 spoonfuls, or 9 cups, and so on.

EXPLANATION OF LINE BLEND TESTING   First, the two dry base glazes (G1 and G3) were mixed in 200-g batches and were scooped into 1-pint (.48-l) plastic containers with 5 oz. (151.35 ml) of water, and shaken up until all the chemicals were blended. Then the glaze G1 Clear was painted on a test tile and identified as Test G1, and G3 Blue was painted on another test tile and identified as Test G3. When fired, these test tiles showed what the base glazes looked like.

Now the line blend testing began: Nine jars, each 1 oz. (30.27 ml), were marked (Test 1, Test 2, Test 3, Test 4, Test 5, Test 6, Test 7, Test 8, Test 9). Test jar 1 was placed on a gram scale, and using a slip trailer to transfer the glaze from container G1 to the test jar, 9 g (90%) of glaze was dripped into the jar. Then 1 g (10%) of G3 was dripped into the

same jar. The two glazes were mixed and painted on a test tile. This process continued with Test 2— by taking 8 g (80%) of G1 and blending it with 2 g (20%) of G3—on through Test 9, incrementally changing the proportions as shown in the chart. These test tiles were then fired to cone 05.

If you see lumps of chemicals floating on top of your liquid glaze, that means it is not thoroughly mixed. For faster and more thorough mixing of the base glazes, you can use an electric kitchen blender. Hot water will also help to dissolve sticky clays and chemicals such as bentonite, macaloid, or gums that do not disperse easily when mixed. You can also screen the glazes through a 50- to 80-mesh sieve. Oxides or stains that are not thoroughly ground can show up on test tiles as spots. To avoid this, use a mortar and pestle to grind the glaze components.

Fluidity Test

Mark your glaze tiles with a line lightly scored into the clay or with a black underglaze pencil, halfway or a third of the way down the test tile. (Use the lower section for marking the cone number, glaze components, glaze number, or firing atmosphere; e.g., *OX* for oxidation, *RE* for reduction.) If the glaze travels past the line during the firing, you can see how much it flowed. It is a good idea to fire your tiles set on end at about a 10-degree angle.

Opacity Test

To test the opacity of your glazes, mark each tile with a dark-colored underglaze pencil prior to glazing and firing. In this way you can observe the opacity of the glaze when fired by noting how clearly the pencil mark shows through the glaze.

1B

Glaze Additives in Relation to Suspension and Application

The quantity and type of glaze additive is related to the composition of the glaze. Testing is essential.

For Glaze Suspension

Components	Percentage
Bentonite (Wyoming)	.5–3
Bentonite (Ferro-purified)	.5–3
Macaloid	.5–2
Vee gum	.5–2
Calcium chloride	.5
Magnesium carbonate	1
Magnesium sulfate (Epsom salts)	.2
Setit A	.5–2
Dextrin	3

Notes:
Bentonite is a sticky clay; 2% is commonly used as a suspending agent to keep glaze components from settling. The purified bentonite has greater suspending properties than the Wyoming.

Macaloid and *vee gum* have greater suspending properties than bentonite, so smaller quantities are needed.

For Glaze Fluidity

Components	Percentage
Darvan #7	.1
Dispersal	.1
Sodium silicate N	.1

Note:
These additives act as deflocculants in glazes that tend to become thixotrophic (viscous). These are useful for glazes that are to be sprayed.

Gums

Components	Percentage
CMC (carboxymethyl-cellulose) gum (synthetic)	1–3
Gum tragacanth (natural gum)*	1–3
Gum arabic*	1–3

Notes:
1% gum is usually added to glazes to delay drying and to alleviate brush drag. It also helps keep glazes, underglaze, engobes, and slips from dusting or crumbling and assists in the suspension of glaze components and the adhesion of glaze to the ware. Gum hardens the glaze surface and, in solution, can be sprayed over oxides or underglazes to keep them from smearing during handling prior to firing.

*Gum tragacanth and gum arabic are natural gums, often used with stains or oxides sensitive to contamination, such as low-fire red and orange glazes with cadmium or selenium stains, unlike CMC gum, which may cause discoloration.

1C

Clay, Slip, and Glaze Recipes from Ceramists

CLAY RECIPES FROM CERAMISTS

A number of ceramists shared the following recipes with us to offer you a wider range of clays, slips, and glazes to test. The Internet provides information on almost every subject in ceramics, from health and safety to glazes to wood firing techniques. There are bulletin boards, newsletters, chat groups, and an opportunity to show work, and most of the ceramics magazines have home pages on the Internet.

The recipes are given in percentages; in some cases, the recipe does not total 100% or exceeds 100%. These small percentage differences will only slightly affect the quantity of the batch by weight. In some cases, we changed the percentages slightly to bring them closer to 100%. We recommend that formulas calling for silica use 325 mesh for glazes and 200 mesh for clays. We did not test any of these formulas. See Chapter 14 in *Hands in Clay* for mixing directions, and remember to observe precautions when mixing glazes.

Ann Roberts, Canada, offers a low-fire talc clay body for sculpture (*Ceramic Review*, vol. 133, 1992).

Low-Fire Talc Clay

Components	Percentage
Ball clay	45.90
Silica (flint)	20.20
Talc	12.20
Whiting	6.10
Gray grog (20 mesh)	15.60
	100.00

The 45.9% ball clay allows the body to remain plastic even with the addition of 15.6% grog to prevent thermal shock during multiple firings.

Mary Parisi, California, offers her modification of Jerry Rothman's recipe for low-shrinkage clay for building thick, solid sculpture walls (up to or exceeding 10 in. [25.40 cm]). Like Rothman, she is able to fire steel in her sculpture without the piece cracking. She says that the different sizes of ione grain grog fill up more space in the clay body than particles of only one size, lessening the shrinkage as well as contributing to the openness of the body. Parisi says, *The clay dries better and fires easier. Bentonite is used to give plasticity, but since it increases shrinkage, it is used in a small amount. . . . The grog can be increased or decreased to reduce graininess or increase plasticity. Water should be carefully controlled; the wetter the clay, the greater amount of shrinkage.*

Cone 06 White Low-Shrinkage Clay

Components	Percentage
C-1 Clay (Pfizer Co.)	14.0
Calcined kaolin	7.0
Talc	7.0
Nepheline syenite	21.0
Ione grain grog #400*	14.0
Ione grain grog #412 or #414*	14.0
Ione grain grog #420*	14.0
Wollastonite	7.0
Bentonite	1.4
Chopped fiberglass (optional)	1.4
	100.8

*Ione grain is no longer available. Substitute w/other types of grogs.

William Daley, Pennsylvania, builds his vessel forms using the following clay body and fires them in oxidation.

Cone 6 Clay

Components	Percentage
Valentine fire clay	20.0
Kentucky ball clay (OM4)	20.0
Fire clay (Missouri)	20.0
Redart Clay	40.0
	100.0

Additive	Percentage
Medium grog	10.0

Gary Holt, California, throws his stoneware clay on the wheel as well as using it to form slab plates. He says that the lightly grogged clay fires to a toasty brown in reduction and is very strong and durable. The white stoneware clay body con-

tains no grog and fires to a gray-white. Holt says, *It throws easily. I use it for both my large slab platters and for functional pieces—casseroles, dinner plates, etc.*

Cone 10 Stoneware

Components	Percentage
IMCO #800 clay	25.0
Fire clay (Kaiser Missouri)	25.0
Kentucky ball clay (OM4)	25.0
Silica 200 mesh (flint)	9.0
Feldspar (Custer)	7.0
Ione grain grog #420	7.0
Talc	2.0
Macaloid (200 mesh)	1.0
	101.0

Cone 10 White Stoneware

Components	Percentage
6-Tile Kaolin	45.0
Feldspar (Custer)	20.0
Silica 200 mesh (flint)	15.0
C-1 clay (Pfizer Co.)	10.0
Kentucky ball clay (OM4)	10.0
Bentonite	1.5
Macaloid	.05
	101.55

Walter Keeler, England, throws his jugs using a clay body consisting of stoneware, ball clay, and sand. He then coats part of the jug with an engobe and salt-glazes the jugs.

Cone 10 Stoneware (for Salt-Glazing)

Components	Percentage
Dorset ball clay	60.72
Staffordshire stoneware clay	30.36
Sand (80 mesh)	9.20
	100.28

Melissa McRaney, California, uses a textured white stoneware clay because her transparent glazes appear true to color against a light-colored background.

Cone 10 White Stoneware

Components	Percentage
Kentucky ball clay (OM4)	25.0
Silica 200 mesh (flint)	20.0
Kaolin (Georgia)	20.0
Feldspar (Custer)	20.0
Macaloid	2.0
Molochite	13.0
	100.0

Karen Massaro, California, contributes a clay recipe along with a compatible glaze recipe (see page 23). These were shared with her when she was a graduate student at the University of Wisconsin, Madison, by Dennis Caffrey, who had studied with Fred Bauer in Seattle—a good example of how information is shared and spreads. Massaro says, *This is a beautiful porcelain surface. Some shrinkage, some crackling. A bit tricky, but interesting for throwing smaller pieces. Very responsive.*

Cone 9 Porcelain

Components	Percentage
Kaolin (EPK)	40.0
Feldspar (Custer)	30.0
Silica	20.0
Nepheline syenite	10.0
	100.0

Frank Boyden, Oregon, says the following porcelain body for wood firing is translucent if thinly thrown. He suggests that for firing in an anagama kiln in which the pieces will be stacked on each other, one should avoid brittle, thin shapes; cylinders do well, as do large, thick, flat plates.

Cones 13–14 Porcelain Clay

Components	Percentage
Kaolin (EPK)	37.50
PV clay	11.25
Feldspar (Custer)	26.25
Silica 200 mesh (flint)	22.50
Pyrophyllite	2.25
Macaloid	.75
	100.50

Bill Roan and Clayton Bailey, California, offer a formula for reprocessing glaze and clay sediment into a clay body. Fire it at your normal studio temperature depending on the firing range of your clay and glazes.

Recycled Clay Body

Components	Percentage
Glaze or clay sediment	50.00
Floor sweepings, sand, or fire clay	50.00
	100.00

SLIP RECIPES FROM CERAMISTS

Gary Holt, California, offers two slips. The white slip is to be used on damp ware, *not on bisque.* The other slip is, Holt says, *particularly well suited for use on a glassy glaze like my Amber glaze. Applied over the glaze, it melts in when fired, giving caramel orange-browns, tans, and occasionally bluish purple.* Since Albany slip is no longer available, you might try a slip mined in Washington called Seattle slip or Sheffield slip from Massachusetts, both offered as substitutes for Albany. This slip recipe came from Jack Troy through Leon Paulos.

Cones 8–10 White Slip (for Damp Ware)

Components	Percentage
Kaolin (EPK)	25.0
Kentucky ball clay (OM4)	25.0
Nepheline syenite	15.0
Talc	7.0
Silica (flint)	20.0
Zircopax	5.0
	97.0

Cones 8–10 Troy Slip

Components	Percentage
Albany slip	75.0
Rutile	10.0
Iron oxide (red)	10.0
Feldspar (Custer)	5.0
	100.0

Note:
Ball-mill for 1–2 hours for even consistency and better flowing characteristics.

Hands in Clay offers the following engobe/slip for stoneware decoration.

Cones 6–10 Stoneware Engobe

Components	Percentage
Kaolin	21.0
Kentucky ball clay (OM4)	21.0
Silica 200 mesh (flint)	29.0
Nepheline syenite	24.0
Borax (powder)	5.0
	100.0

Colorants/Additives	Percentage
Red: iron	6.0
Blue: cobalt	2.0
Green: chrome	3.0

Patrick Siler, Washington, stencils black and white images on greenware using these slips. Then, before single-firing to cone 5, he covers the slip with a sprayed-on clear glaze.

Cone 5 Black Slip

Components	Percentage
Fire clay (Lincoln)	66.6
Kentucky ball clay (OM4)	33.3
	99.9

Colorants/Additives	Percentage
Black stain	15.0
Iron oxide (red)	15.0

Cone 5 Ivory Slip

Components	Percentage
Fire clay (Lincoln)	33.3
Kaolin	33.3
Kentucky ball clay (OM4)	33.3
	99.9

Walter Keeler, England, applies an engobe to the lower part of his salt-glazed jugs in order to achieve a contrast between the characteristic "orange peel" salt-glaze surface and the smooth engobe. He then

sprays on color mixed with a little engobe to prevent it from brushing off the unfired pot when it is handled. He salt-glazes, firing to 2336°F/1280°C (Orton cone 10), salts at 2280°F/1250°C (Orton cone 9), then soaks for half an hour.

Engobe for Salt Glaze

Components	Percentage
Feldspar	60.0
Kaolin	40.0
	100.0 .

Colorants/Additives
Mixtures of oxides and/or stains—for example, chrome oxide and cobalt oxide
Black stain
Black stain and cobalt or manganese dioxide and iron

Ericka Clark Shaw, California, offers a crackle slip that she says *can be applied over green or bisque ware, either under or over a glaze.*

Crackle Slip

Components	Percentage
Nepheline syenite	50.0
Magnesium carbonate	50.0
	100.0

Colorants/Additives
Gum for working consistency
Stains for color (except lilac)

Jim Gremel, California, forms his raku vessels in plaster molds cast from a special slip-casting body. Gremel says, *I switched from throwing to slip-casting about four years ago. The cast pieces survive the raku process much better than their predecessors, and their color development seems to be better.*

Cone 07 Raku Slip-Casting Body

Components	Percentage
Imco #400 fire clay	27.02
Tennessee ball clay	27.02
Feldspar (Custer)	13.52
Ione grain #65 F grog (very fine powder)	16.22
Mullite 100 mesh	16.22
	100.00

Additives
45.95 lb. (20.86 kg) of water and 351.36 g of Darvan #7 deflocculant per 100-lb. (45.40-kg) batch. Additional water, Darvan #7, and sodium silicate N are added as needed to achieve a specific gravity reading of about 1.75. It is important to bisque-fire the clay to cone 06 before raku-firing.

Richard Hirsch, New York, uses terra sigillata combined with low-fire glazes to develop the rich patina of his vessel forms. He colors his white terra sigillata with stains, then may intermix the terra sigillatas themselves. He says that the firing limit for good color is cone 04 and that the color values can be changed by varying the percentages of the stain in the white base. The frit helps in hardness and color.

White Terra Sigillata

Components	Percentage
Kentucky (OM4) or Tenn. #5 ball clay	20.0
Frit 3110	.5
Water (H$_2$O)	80.0
Calgon*	1.0
	101.5

*The active ingredient in Calgon is sodium carbonate

Colorants/Additives	Percentage
Medium blue: Medium blue stain	10.0
Medium green: Medium green stain	10.0
Orange: Saturn orange stain	10.0
Purple: Red and medium blue sigillatas mixed	

Red Terra Sigillata

Components	Percentage
Kentucky ball clay (OM4)	50.0
Iron oxide (red)	50.0
Calgon*	5.0
	105.0

Additive	
Water (H$_2$O)	61.0 g

*The active ingredient in Calgon is sodium carbonate.

GLAZE RECIPES FROM CERAMISTS

Low- to Mid-Range Glazes

Richard Hirsch, New York, uses a low-fire cone 04 base glaze to which he adds a variety of colorants to create semiopaque glazes that interface well with the terra sigillata beneath, creating a patina and layering effect. The cone 04 limit ensures good color.

Cone 04 Base Glaze (for Use with Terra Sigillatas)

Components	Percentage
Colemanite (Gerstley borate)	31.54
Lithium carbonate	8.30
Nepheline syenite	4.15
Kaolin (EPK)	4.15
Silica 200 mesh (flint)	34.86
Whiting	16.60
	99.60

Colorants/Additives	Percentage
Blue-green: leave out lithium, add copper carbonate	4.0
Yellow-blue-green:	
Copper carbonate	4.0
Rutile	4.0
Red-rust:	
Rutile	10.0
Golden ambrosia stain	3.0
Orange-rust:	
Iron oxide (red)	6.0
Rutile	4.0
Saturn orange stain	2.0

The Richmond Art Center, California, uses a raku glaze that develops a coppery luster. Ceramic instructor Larry Henderson says, *After the glaze bubbles and then flattens out and turns glossy, I take the pots out and place them in a covered garbage can with sawdust for 10 minutes, then remove them from the can and spray them with water.*

Cones 09–07 Clear Raku Glaze

Components	Percentage
Colemanite (Gerstley borate)	79.0
Nepheline syenite	21.0
	100.0

Colorants/Additives for Black/Copper Luster	Percentage
Iron oxide (red)	4.0
Cobalt	2.5
Copper carbonate	3.0

The Richmond Art Center, California, also contributes a white crackle raku glaze. To achieve a green color, they brush on a copper carbonate solution over the glaze and fire in oxidation. When fired under reduction the same colorant turns into a copper luster.

White Crackle Raku Glaze

Components	Percentage
Frit 3134	54.00
Kaolin (EPK)	20.68
Silica 325 mesh (flint)	20.68
Bentonite	2.58
Zircopax or tin oxide	2.06
	100.00

Steven Branfman, Massachusetts, offers a reliable glossy raku base glaze that he fires to cone 08. The glaze is a beautiful blue with flashes of copper and other colors. To encourage color development, Branfman allows his pots to oxidize for 15–20 seconds after they are removed from the raku kiln and placed into a metal can containing sawdust. When flames begin to lick over the edge of the pots, the lid is placed over the can to allow the ware to smoke.

Cone 05 Aqua Variation #1

Components	Percentage
Gerstley borate	80.0
Cornwall stone	20.0
	100.0

Colorants/Additives	Percentage
Tin oxide	2.0
Cobalt carbonate	2.0
Vanadium (pentoxide) or vanadium-based Mason stains	3.0

Roslyn Myers, New York, contributes a low-fire texture glaze to which she adds silicon carbide, molochite, steel and brass shavings, and so on, in order to produce unusual textures.

Cone 05 Low-Fire Texture Glaze

Components	Percentage
Borax (powder)	30.0
Kaolin (Georgia)	10.0
Feldspar (Custer)	20.0
Soda ash	18.0
Silica 325 mesh (flint)	20.0
Bentonite	2.0
	100.0

Colorants/Additives

For varying texture effects on white clay, use .5–1.5% of the following materials, either sprinkled over the tile or mixed in the glaze:

Silicon carbide (36–100 grit)—white background, widely spaced dark gray texture
Silica sand (30–60 mesh)—30 mesh gives white texture, large granules
Ilmenite (granulated)—small brown granules catch the light and give golden sparkles
Ione grain #420—very rough gray texture
Molochite—similar to silica sand, but smaller white granules, overall texture
Steel grindings—very rough, shiny, black lava effect
Stainless steel grindings—particles do not melt and flow at cone 05, leaving sharp tooth, dark gray
Brass—mottled light and dark green, flows but clear spaces remain

Hands in Clay offers two more cone 05 glazes. The clear glaze fires to a clear gloss over white clay and fires clear glossy with a white granulated mottle when applied over red clay.

Hands in Clay Cone 05 Clear Glaze

Components	Percentage
Gerstley borate (or Leslie Ceramics Akiko borate)	65.0
Kaolin (Georgia)	15.0
Silica 325 mesh (flint)	18.0
Bentonite	2.0
	100.0

Notes:
On white clay body—clear gloss
On red clay body—white granulated mottle

For a clear 05 crackle glaze, eliminate the copper carbonate used as colorant in the green crackle glaze. For other colors, test it with glaze stains instead of the copper.

Hands in Clay Cone 05 Green Crackle Glaze

Components	Percentage
Frit #25	80.96
Kaolin (Georgia)	12.38
Bentonite	1.90
Copper carbonate	4.76
	100.00

Notes:
On cone 05 white clay body—blue-green, medium crackle
On cone 05 red body—dark olive green, medium crackle
On cone 5 clay body—olive green, transparent with small crackles
On porcelain at cone 5—at this temperature, the glaze runs

Medium-Range Glazes

Susanne Ashmore, Canada, offers a glaze from Emanuel Cooper's *The Potter's Book of Glaze Recipes.* She finds it an excellent base glaze for overlap experiments with other glazes and fires it at a wide range of temperatures, from cone 05 to cone 8. Of Richard Zakin's glaze, Ashmore says: *I found this in* Electric Kiln Ceramics *by Richard Zakin. I fire with an electric kiln, so these two glazes have been tested only under those conditions. I do try to achieve long soaking periods at cone 6 to cone 7.*

Emanuel Cooper's Cones 05–8 Clear Base Glaze

Components	Percentage
Feldspar (Kona F-4)	38.0
Whiting	14.0
Zinc oxide	12.0
Kentucky ball clay (OM4)	6.0
Silica (flint)	30.0
	100.0

Richard Zakin's Medium-Range Glaze

Components	Percentage
Nepheline syenite	40.0
Dolomite	18.0
Silica (flint)	18.0
Kaolin	12.0
Bone ash	6.0
Lithium carbonate	2.0
Zinc oxide	4.0
	100.0

Colorant/Additive	Percentage
Copper carbonate	2

To add more medium-range glazes, *Hands in Clay* tested some cone 5 and cone 6 glazes, one of which is an example of how radically a glaze may vary when fired in oxidation or in reduction. For this reason, the matt glaze is called "Night and Day."

Cone 5 "Night and Day" Matt Glaze

Components	Percentage
Dolomite	18.0
Gerstley borate (or Leslie Ceramics Akiko borate)	10.0
Feldspar (Kona F-4)	15.0
Nepheline syenite	23.0
Kentucky ball clay (OM4)	18.0
Silica (flint)	10.0
Titanium dioxide	6.0
	100.0

Notes:
Oxidation—pale warm yellow gloss glaze
Reduction—handsome granite gray, dry matt

Cone 5 Japanese Wood Ash Glaze

Components	Percentage
Ash	16.0
Silica (flint)	33.0
Feldspar (Custer)	21.0
Colemanite (Gerstley borate)	4.0
Kentucky ball clay (OM4)	7.0
Dolomite	10.0
Iron oxide (Spanish red)	9.0
	100.0

Notes:
Oxidation—reddish brown, pebbly
Reduction—rich, glossy brown-black
At cone 10—matt, purplish

Hands in Clay Cone 6 Matt Glaze (Oxidation)

Components	Percentage
Feldspar (Custer)	33.0
Gerstley borate	5.0
Silica 325 mesh (flint)	25.0
Whiting	24.0
Kaolin (Georgia)	11.0
Bentonite	2.0
	100.0

Note:
A buttery white, translucent matt glaze with no toxic ingredients; good for the inside of food containers

Lourdan Kimbrell, California, offers a lavender-violet satin matt glaze and a periwinkle blue glaze that can be fired in an electric or gas kiln. When the lavender-violet glaze is fired in a gas kiln, a more reducing atmosphere will cause it to turn from a lavender to burgundy color. Increasing the amount of magnesium carbonate in the periwinkle glaze will turn it from a periwinkle to a darker violet-purple color.

Cones 4–6 Lavender-Violet Satin Matt Glaze

Components	Percentage
Potash feldspar*	32.6
Magnesium carbonate	2.3
Wollastonite	23.0
Silica 325 mesh (flint)	42.1
	100.0

Colorant/Additive	Percentage
Cobalt oxide	1.0

*Use any potash type of feldspar.

Cones 4–6 Periwinkle Blue-Purple Glaze

Components	Percentage
Frit 25	44.4
Lithium carbonate	5.2
Whiting	14.0
Kaolin	9.1
Silica 325 mesh (flint)	27.3
	100.0

Colorant/Additive	Percentage
Magnesium carbonate	1–5*

*Increasing the percentage of magnesium carbonate will result in a more violet-colored glaze.

High-Fire Glazes

Gary Holt, California, uses the following high-fire glaze mainly on stoneware. *On my stoneware, with a medium to heavy reduction it will fire to a honey brown color. Takes iron oxide decoration well. It will craze on white stoneware or porcelain.*

Cones 9–10 Amber Glaze

Components	Percentage
Feldspar (Custer)	52.00
Whiting	18.25
Silica (flint)	16.75
Kaolin (EPK)	10.00
Tin oxide	1.30
Rutile	1.70
	100.00

Frank Boyden, Oregon, applies this Shino-type glaze to porcelain, which he fires to high temperature in his wood-fired anagama kiln. Boyden says, *This is not my own glaze, but Tom Coleman's, I think. I use it along with many others. Most Shino glazes will fire extremely high.* He recommends avoiding delicate brushwork and strong stains containing cobalt, chrome, and copper.

Cones 13–14 Shino-Type Glaze

Components	Percentage
Feldspar (Kona F-4)	15.0
Spodumene	13.0
Soda ash	3.0
Nepheline syenite	50.0
Kentucky ball clay (OM4)	16.0
Kaolin (EPK)	3.0
	100.0

Colorant/Additive	Percentage
Iron oxide (red)	.125–.25

Karen Massaro, California, sends a clear glaze that came originally from Fred Bauer. It is compatible with the clay-body recipe she gave earlier (see page 17), and she says it is good in oxidation or in reduction. *For celadon, you may add 1–3% iron oxide to yield a lovely blue-green color.* Of the barium matt glaze, Massaro says, *Colorants can be added singly or in combination. Results are interesting; the richer hues with varied undertones come when using two or more oxides. A single oxide gives a flatter color.*

Cones 9–10 Clear Glaze

Components	Percentage
Silica (flint)	14.56
Cornwall stone	66.37
Whiting	12.41
Colemanite	2.49
Zinc oxide	2.49
Magnesium carbonate (or 2% bentonite)	1.72
	100.04

Colorants/Additives	Percentage
Iron oxide (red)	2–5
Copper carbonate	1–5
Nickel oxide	1–3
Manganese dioxide	2–8

Cone 10 Dry Barium* Matt Glaze (Not for Food Containers)

Components	Percentage
Nepheline syenite	44.93
Kentucky ball clay (OM4)	6.69
Barium carbonate (**toxic**)	35.37
Rutile	8.60
Flint	2.61
Bentonite	1.91
	100.11

*Toxic material

Cones 8–10 Matt Black Glaze

Components	Percentage
Nepheline syenite	17.51
Dolomite	13.98
Cornwall stone	25.23
Whiting (calcium)	3.80
Talc	14.36
Kaolin	21.50
Silica 325 mesh (flint)	3.83
	100.21

Colorants/Additives (Add All for Black)	Percentage
Iron chromate	4.00
Iron oxide (red)	6.01
Cobalt oxide	2.00
Nickel oxide	2.00
Ilmenite (powder)	3.51
Bentonite	2.00

Ernst Haüsermann, Switzerland, glazed the bowl shown in Figure 13-3 in *Hands in Clay* with the following simple ash glaze fired to 2462°F/1350°C. It fires on stoneware to a matt, clear gray. Haüsermann's feldspar comes from Norway and is similar to Custer feldspar. The ashes he uses in his glazes come from the wood he burns in his ceramic-tile heating stove.

Ash Glaze

Components	Percentage
K-feldspar	30.0
Mixed ash	30.0
Kaolin	26.0
White stoneware clay	14.0
	100.0

Harris Deller, Illinois, says, *A heavy reduction beginning at cone 010 all the way to a hot cone 10 is very important for this cone 10 Chun celadon glaze. I clear the kiln atmosphere at the end of the firing for 5 to 10 minutes by oxidizing.*

Cone 10 Chun Celadon Glaze

Components	Percentage
Feldspar* potash	37.1–42.1*
Kaolin	1.8
Silica* (flint)	27.2–32.2*
Whiting	2.6
Colemanite	8.8
Dolomite	8.8
Zinc oxide	1.7
Barium carbonate (**toxic**)	4.4
Iron oxide (red)	2.6
	95–105

Colorants/Additives	Percentage
Green-blue: Spanish red iron oxide[†]	1.5
Green: Spanish red iron oxide	2–3
Red: Copper carbonate	.50

*Adjustments may be made in feldspar and/or flint to control crazing. (Custer feldspar is a potash spar.)

[†]Deller says, *I use Spanish red iron oxide because it's a finer-mesh iron with a good consistency from batch to batch. Some red iron oxide, because of larger particle size, will cause the glaze to have freckles or iron spots. Since this glaze contains [toxic] barium, it should not be used on the interior of food containers, and you should protect yourself against exposure to barium when mixing it.*

William S. Holoway, California, offers a purple semimatt glaze, saying, *This glaze must be screened and mixed thoroughly to ensure a smooth consistency and must be applied relatively thick to ensure a good all-over violet to purple.* This glaze is stable and will hardly drip or move in the kiln.

Cone 8 Purple Semimatt

Components	Percentage
Nepheline syenite	22.5
Colemanite (Gerstley borate)	12.1
Wollastonite	6.8
Macaloid	6.4
Dolomite	5.4
Kentucky ball clay (OM4)	11.3
Silica (flint)	35.3
	99.8

Colorant/Additive	Percentage
Cobalt	3.0

After mixing her cone 8 crystalline glaze, **Kate Malone, England,** passes it through a 120-mesh sieve and applies it thickly to bisqued ware. To grow glaze crystals, she programs her kiln to rise at a specific rate, hold (soak), and cool. Malone fires her work up to 2300°F/1260°C and then cools the kiln as quickly as possible to about 1995°F/1090°C. Then she soaks the ware in stages: first at 1995°F/1090°C for 3 hours, 1963°F/1073°C for 1½ hours, 1956°F/1069°C for 1 hour, 1904°F/1049°C for ½ hour, and then she turns the kiln off. Malone says, *The glaze is very fluid at 2300°F/1260°C. Each piece has to have a bespoke tray and stilt and grinding of the base after firing.*

Cone 8 Crystalline Glaze Base

Components	Percentage
Ferro frit 3110	44.0
Zinc oxide	26.4
Flint	20.4
Titanium dioxide	7.6
Kaolin	1.2
	99.60

Colorants/Additives	Percentage
Add the following chemicals to the base glaze:	
Soft green: Copper carbonate	2.0
Golden honey crystals: Iron oxide (red)	3.0
Soft gray blue: Cobalt carbonate	0.4
Manganese dioxide	1.2
Stronger blue: Cobalt carbonate	2.0
Manganese dioxide	2.0
Black: Vanadium pentoxide	3.2
Nickel oxide	1.2

Sun Chao, Taiwan, offers a formula with a wide range of color possibilities based on variations that can be made in the proportions of the glaze chemicals. Chao fires the glaze in an oxidation atmosphere at 2372°F/1300°C and then drops the temperature to 2012°F/1100°C, where he holds it for 4½ hours. Any oxides can be added to the Aqua Variation #1 formula in increments from 1–10%.

Cone 9 Aqua Variation #1 Crystalline Glaze

Components	Percentage
Ferro frit 3110	45.0–50.0
Zinc oxide	20.0–25.0
Silica	9.0–10.0
Kaolin	1.0
Titanium dioxide	2.0–8.0
Bentonite	2.0
	79.00–96.00

Colorants/Additives	Percentage
Various oxides	1–10

Cone 10 Porcelain Slip

Components	Percentage
Kaolin (Grolleg)	53.94
Feldspar (Custer)	19.60
Silica (flint)	11.76
Pyrophyllite	12.74
Bentonite	1.96
	100.00

Colorants/Additives	Percentage
Flesh: Cerium oxide	8.0
Rutile	1.5
Pink-gray: Rutile	8.0
Iron chromate	5.0
Bleeding blue: Cobalt carbonate	1.5
Copper carbonate	4.0

Cone 10 Blue Pearly Slip

Components	Percentage
Ball clay	23.85
Fire clay	11.00
Feldspar (Custer)	27.54
Silica (flint)	22.95
Rutile	13.75
Cobalt carbonate	.91
	100.00

Vapor-Firing Glazes

Peter Coussoulis, California, offers a sodium vapor formula he uses when firing ware in his updraft 30-cu. ft. (.85-cu.-m) salt kiln. When the kiln reaches cone 8, Coussoulis sprays the sodium solution (using a hand-pump garden sprayer) into each of his two kiln ports. This is followed by throwing 3 to 4 lb. (1,362 to 1,816 g) of salt into the ports. This process continues every 15 minutes, until the kiln reaches cone 10. Coussoulis suggests the following proportions for this mixture.

Cones 8–10 Sodium Vapor Mixture

Components	Solution
Soda ash	3–4 lb. (1,362–1,816 g)
Water	2½ gal. (9.47 l)

Coussoulis uses various slips and colorants for his low-salt firing.

Larry Henderson, California, uses this glaze with salt-glaze firing. It requires a strong dose of salt to make it shiny. Because salt vapor does not penetrate the inside of pots readily, to achieve full gloss, use glaze only on the outside of objects.

Cones 8–10 Salt Glaze

Components	Percentage
Feldspar (Custer)	53.41
Wollastonite	10.90
Gerstley borate	5.45
Silica (flint)	22.89
Kentucky ball clay (OM4)	5.45
Bentonite	2.18
	100.28

Colorants/Additives	Percentage
Iron oxide (red)	4.36
Cobalt	0.55

Tony Yeh, Taiwan, receives inspiration from the thoughts of Chinese philosophers Lao-tze and Chuang-tze. They felt that nature should be the prism through which people view life and work. Their views have influenced Yeh's ceramics and choice of glazes. He offers a high-fire rutile glaze fired under reduction to cones 8–9.

Cones 8–9 Rutile Rabbit's Fur Glaze

Components	Percentage
Whiting	18.89
Zinc oxide	5.56
Feldspar	51.42
Ball clay	8.39
Kaolin	15.74
	100.00

Colorants/Additives	Percentage
Iron oxide (red)	4.62
Rutile	9.23

1D

Percentage Charts: Clays, Chemicals, Feldspars, Wood Ash, Frits, and Opacifiers

Chemical Composition of Kaolins

Brand	Percentage										Alka-line	Ig Loss	MnO	Misc. trace alkalies	F_2	V_2O_5
	SiO_2	AL_2O_3	Fe_2O_3	CaO	MgO	TiO_2	K_2O	Na_2O	$P_2O_5\&F$	SO_3						
Kaolex D-6 Kaolin	45.4	39.0	.6			1.5						13.32				
Kingsley Kaolin	45.1	38.5	.4			1.6						13.90				
McNamee Kaolin	44.46	39.34	.33	.06	.05	1.20	.31	.04				13.99				
Snocal 707 Kaolin	65.41	23.12	.20	.31	.14	.20	.44	.02				10.20				
AJAX P Kaolin	45.20	38.08	.45	.26	.30	1.52	.04	.02				12.51				
Delta Kaolin	46.2	37.7	.40	.04	.05	2.1				.1		13.10		.3		
EPK Kaolin	46.5	37.62	.51	.25	.16	.36	.40	.02	.19			14.00			.08	.0001
Grolleg, English Kaolin	48.0	37.0	.07	.10	.30	.03	1.90	.10				12.10				
Kaopaque 20 Kaolin	45.20	39.20										13.92				
Laguna #1 Kaolin	45.48	38.70	.40	.06	trace	1.43	.18	trace				13.82				
Sapphire Kaolin	45.50	37.70	.80	.20	.15	1.40	.19	.10				13.50				

(continued)

Chemical Composition of Kaolins *(continued)*

Brand	SiO$_2$	AL$_2$O$_3$	Fe$_2$O$_3$	CaO	MgO	TiO$_2$	K$_2$O	Na$_2$O	P$_2$O$_5$&F	SO$_3$	Alka-line	Ig Loss	MnO	Misc. trace alkalies	F$_2$	V$_2$O$_5$
Georgia Kaolin	44.40	38.90	.40	.10	.10	1.30	.20	.20				14.21				
Standard porcelain (English)	48.0	37.00	.68	.07	.30	.02	1.65	.10				12.50				
Super standard porcelain (English)	47.0	38.00	.39	.10	.22	.03	.80	.15				13.00				
AJAX-SC calcined Kaolin 325 M	55.80	44.40										.80				
Glomax LL calcined Kaolin 325	52.80	44.60	.40		.20	1.60	.10	.30				.80				
T-7 Kaolin	44.72	39.20	.36	.22	.01	1.76		.01	.10	.02		13.55	.01			
#6 Tile Kaolin	46.90	38.20	.35	.43	.53	1.42		.04				13.90				
Ione Kaolin	43.50	54.00	.50									N/A				

Chemical Composition of Fire Clays

Brand	SiO$_2$	AL$_2$O$_3$	Fe$_2$O$_3$	CaO	MgO	TiO$_2$	K$_2$O	Na$_2$O	P$_2$O$_5$&F	SO$_3$	Alka-line	Ig Loss	MnO	Misc. trace alkalies
IMCO 400 fire clay	49.6	34.4	2.57	.04	.56		1.10	.06				11.70		
IMCO 800 fire clay	49.6	31.5	6.44	.04	.50		.92	.10				10.8		
Lincoln 60 fire clay	52.0	29.0	2.0				1.9					12.4		
Hawthorne Bond fire clay	55.10	39.11	1.02	.15	.85	2.08	1.24	.24	.09	.03		11.32		
Greenstripe 200 M fire clay	54.10	27.98	3.58									11–12		
A.P. Green 28 M fire clay	52.00	31.0	2.0	.04	.04	2.0	.10	.10				11.00		
Cedar Heights fire clay	63.70	21.13	1.62	.55	.11	.30		.47	.07			8.24		
Goldart 200 mesh fire clay	57.33	28.50	1.23	.08	.22	1.96	1.18	1.16		.24		10.03		
Missouri fire clay	53.41	30.41	1.61									11.22		
Pinelake fire clay	70.40	24.80	1.35	.27	.29	2.03	.86	.86		.17		N/A		

Chemical Composition of Ball Clays

Brand	Percentage										Alka-line	Ig Loss	MnO	Alkalies	C
	SiO_2	AL_2O_3	Fe_2O_3	CaO	MgO	TiO_2	K_2O	Na_2O	$P_2O_5\&F$	SO_3					
Kentucky Special ball clay	49.64	29.33	.95	.29	.25	1.48	1.0	16.81				16.81			
Kentucky ball clay (OM4)	51.92	31.78	.87	.21	.19	1.52	.89	.38				12.29			
Old Hickory #5 ball clay	58.56	26.17	1.04	.08	.22	1.50	.89	.12				10.65			
Taylor ball clay	62.90	23.70	1.07	.09		1.58	.35	.09				9.58			
Bandy ball clay	61.0	24.54	.99	.09	.12	1.29	1.69	.36	.07	.11		9.74	.01		
Champion and Challenger ball clay	55.60	28.38	.98	.37	.30	1.64	.40	.12	.15	.03		12.30	.02		
Coppen Light ball clay	58.33	26.95	1.14	.12	.22	1.57	.64	.08	.13	.04		10.52	.12		
Dresden ball clay	52.5	30.6	1.5			1.1						12.4		1.9	
CP-7 ball clay	54.89	28.67	31.0	.3	.1	1.6	.26	.05				12.53			
Foundry Hill Cream	66.21	20.48					.67	.55				12.09			
Tennessee ball clay #1	49.08	34.02	.85	.30	trace	1.51	.35	.09				9.58			
Gold Label 200 M	61.69	22.09	1.35	.13	.42	1.16	1.17	.10				9.21			
Kentucky Stone 200 M	66.40	21.40	1.60	.20	.50	1.30	1.30	.20		.16					.34
Black Charm ball clay	62.96	22.66	1.53	.33	.12	.20	1.34	.32	.04	.11		10.52	.05		
Jackson ball clay	54.90	30.0	1.00	.30	.40	1.70	.30	.10				11.30			

Chemical Composition of Red Clays

Brand	Percentage										Alka-line	Ig Loss	MnO	Misc. trace alkalies
	SiO_2	AL_2O_3	Fe_2O_3	CaO	MgO	TiO_2	K_2O	Na_2O	$P_2O_5\&F$	SO_3				
Laterite red clay	32.5	29.3	24.0	.3	1.5	1.5						11.3		
Redart clay	64.27	16.41	7.04	.23	1.55	1.06	4.07	.40				4.92		
Red Horse clay	67.46	21.99	6.61	.45	.62		1.20	.30				1.18		

Chemical Composition of Miscellaneous Clays and Chemicals

Brand	Percentage																	
	SiO_2	AL_2O_3	Fe_2O_3	CaO	MgO	TiO_2	K_2O	Na_2O	$P_2O_5\&F$	SO_3	Alkaline	Ig Loss	MnO	Alkalies	FeO	H_2	$KNaO$	B_2O_3
Roseville stoneware clay	60.87	23.41	2.13	.37	.21	1.65	2.51	.31		.03		8.51						
Salt Lick stoneware clay	62.0	25.0	1.60	.20	.50	1.50	2.30	.10				6.80						
Laguna borate	18.7	8.10	.10	18.9	2.3	.10	1.4	4.0										27.5
Wollastonite	50.0	1.00	1.00	47.0		1.00						N/A						
Blackbird (Barnard) clay	61.0	25.54										9.74						
Bentonite	63.02	21.08	3.25	.65	2.67		2.57	2.57				5.15				5.64	2.90	
Pyrophyllite	73.00	20.40	.50			.50	.20					3.50			.35			
C-1 clay	75.6	15.8	.04	.8	.5	.10	1.55	.50				4.84						
Jordan clay	67.19	20.23	1.73									6.89		2.23				
Kentucky stone clay	66.40	21.40	1.60	.20	.50	1.30	1.30	.20				7.6						
Gerstley borate	10.0	1.8	.20	22.0	3.5			.25	4.5									29.0
PV clay	75.9	14.8	.10	.80			6.0					1.90						
Velvacast	45.40	38.70	.30	.10	.20	1.40		trace	.10			13.80						
Volcanic ash	72.0	13.0	.70	.70	.10	.10	5.0	4.5										
Saggar clay	59.40	27.20	.70	.60	.20	1.6	.70	.30				9.40						
Kyanite	38.65	61.80	.94	.05	.06	.95						8.60			.42			
Molochite	52.50	43.00	1.00	.10	.10	.08	1.50	.10										
Cady Cal 100	.70	2.3		25.3	.30													48.6
Talc, Nytol 100 HR	55.55	.30	.20	8.0	30.10			.30				3.46						

Chemical Composition of Feldspars

Brand	Percentage														
	SiO_2	Al_2O_3	Fe_2O_3	CaO	MgO	TiO_2	K_2O	Na_2O	$P_2O_5\&F$	SO_3	Alka-line	Ig Loss	MnO	Misc. trace alkalies	Li_2O
Custer feldspar	68.65	17.54	.08	.30			10.43	3.0							
Kona F-4 feldspar	66.76	19.70	.04	1.80			4.80	6.90							
Spodumene	60.98	27.87	.45	1.50	.61		.51	.22							6.55
Nepheline syenite	60.24	24.05	.06	.15	.02		5.00	10.2							
G-200 feldspar	66.05	19.41		1.10			10.32	3.12							
Kingman feldspar	66.29	18.80					12.28	2.63							
Cornwall stone	72.86	16.43		2.55			5.01	3.15							
Unispar 50	66.8	19.6	.04	1.70			4.8	6.9							
Spodumene LM	50–55	26–28	.07–.3				.1–.5	.1–.5	8–10				.02–.4		7.1–7.5

Chemical Composition of Wood Ash

Type	Percentage												
	SiO_2	Al_2O_3	Fe_2O_3	CaO	MgO	TiO_2	K_2O	Na_2O	$P_2O_5\&F$	SO_3	Alkaline	Ig Loss	MnO
Walnut	16.0	.50	1.90	38.7	6.60		14.70	4.90	6.50				.42
Pine	10.0	.40	4.0	25.0	6.30		26.50	8.60	8.90				5.60
Oak	15.30	.10	2.40	30.0	12.0		14.0	9.12	13.10				.10
Apple	2.65	1.98	.70	54.20	3.25		.89	4.90	1.60				34.70

Chemical Composition of Leadless Frits

Brand Number	Na$_2$O	Na$_2$F$_2$	NaKO	K$_2$O	Li$_2$O	CaO	CaF$_2$	CdO	ZnO	SO$_3$	B$_2$O$_3$	Al$_2$O$_3$	SiO$_2$	F	Sb$_2$O$_3$	MgO	ZrO$_2$	SRO	Expansion
F15				3.6							23.0	3.8	57.0						4.42
F43	11.20			.50		8.0					22.5	9.5	48.30						8.22
F79	4.0			1.20	.50	4.8					26.5	9.0	53.0					1.0	5.72
F499	21.0										28.4	7.20	43.4						9.46
F10	13.5			5.50		2.5					12.0	8.50	45.0				13.0		8.74
F125	10.9			2.0		7.0					21.5		43.6				15.0		7.01
F326	6.0			2.30		4.5					10.6	8.6	56.5			1.5	10.0		6.60
F18	2.6			2.4		11.8					8.9	6.8	59.5					8.0	7.13
F38	5.5					4.2					15.0	4.2	53.10				1.20	16.8	6.18
F300	2.7			1.8		10.0					5.0	10.1	62.4					8.2	7.29
F502	2.2			1.0		12.1					9.5	5.8	61.10					8.3	6.43
F506				4.0		13.5					7.0	10.5	60.5					4.5	7.32
F69											30.2	12.5	44.5			12.8			3.96
F498	3.6					15.5					16.6	10.5	43.8			10.0			8.92
FZ14	10.0			3.0		6.5			10.0		5.0	14.0	51.5						9.53
FZ390	8.2					2.0				.85	18.5	5.5	65.0						5.84
KGF 4171	12.68					11.07					21.64		54.61						
KGF 4194	12.70			5.90		2.40					14.5	9.20	55.30						
KGF 9002	7.01			4.33		9.76			7.0		15.76	5.53	45.39				5.23		
KGF 4616	3.40			1.50		4.60					10.30	4.50	43.70						
KG 4101	13.03			5.32		2.23					13.23	8.52	51.71	10.3					

Chemical Composition of Leadless Frits

Type	Percentage															
	Na_2O	Na_2F_2	NaKO	K_2O	Li_2O	CaO	CaF_2	CdO	ZnO	SO_3	B_2O_3	Al_2O_3	SiO_2	F	Sb_2O_3	MgO
P-25	14.70			5.40		.50			.70		16.90	12.10	49.70	1.80		
P-283	16.30					.30						5.90	76.50			.70
3124	5.60			.60		14.50					12.50	10.00	56.80			
3134	10.20					20.10					23.20		46.50			
3195	5.70					11.30					22.40	12.00	48.50			
2106		21.67				3.42			3.60		13.00	9.13	45.20		3.98	
3110	15.3			2.3		6.3					2.6	3.7	69.8			
3269	11.1			8.1		.10			1.0		15.2	13.2	49.7	1.6		
3270	8.6			5.5		9.4					16.5	8.6	51.4			
3278	15.3					6.9					21.6		54.6			
5301	19.2			5.1		2.3					11.7	11.3	41.8	8.6		

Notes:
This table offers a selection of leadless frits. The numbers of equivalent frits that can be substituted are listed in the following table.

Brands and Numbers of Equivalent* Leadless Frits

Brand	FERRO	FUSION	O-Hommel	PEMCO	Glostex	Dal-Tile
	3134	F-12	14 (242)	P-54	GF 111	F-201
	3269	F-225	25 (259)	P-25		
	3124	F-19	90	P-311	GF 113	F-90
	3110	F-75		P-1505	GF 134	
	3195					F-434
Frit	3278		K-3	P-830		F-259
Number	3249			P-1409		
	CC-268		630	P-786		
	3289		400	P-626		
	3270		378	P-802		
	3269	FZ-25	259	P-25	GF 114	F-392
	3293			P-283		

*Although comparable frits are considered equivalents by manufacturers, they often result in slight variations when directly substituted. It is recommended that all frit substitutes be tested.

Percentage Composition of Opacifiers

Opacifier	Percentage						
	ZrO_2	$ZrSiO_4$	SiO_2	TiO_2	Fe_2O_3	AL_2O_3	Other Components
Zircopax		96.00		0.25	0.10		
Ultrox	65.00		35.00				
Superpax		93.40		0.25	0.10		
Zircon G milled		98.60		0.20	0.04		
Calcium zirconium silicate	50.50		26.70				CaO 18.80
Magnesium zirconium silicate	53.60		27.50				MgO 17.40
Zinc zirconium silicate	46.40		24.20				ZnO 28.60

1E

Chemicals and Materials

This list includes the main oxides used in glaze forming and coloring as well as the materials that yield them. Colorants and opacifiers are listed separately.

Use all of these materials with great care and proper protection. The precautions that should be taken when using all ceramics materials are discussed in Chapter 10 of *Hands in Clay*. **The bold letter in front of each material indicates its degree of toxicity.** All chemicals, even those rated **N** for nuisance should be handled with care. A respirator and gloves should be worn at all times when using these and all other chemicals. Some chemicals with an **N** or even an **H** rating such as for clays, are nontoxic, however silica in the dust or other minerals inhaled from any of these materials can accumulate in your lungs over a period of time and can cause silicosis, respiratory problems, or other disorders. Be aware also of the type of gloves you wear; individuals allergic to latex should wear vinyl or nonlatex gloves, or vice versa. However, new findings may change these ratings, so it is important that you keep up to date on current information. See Chapter 5A for sources of information on health and safety.

H = highly toxic

M = moderately toxic

S = slightly toxic

N = nuisance

H alumina (aluminum) (Al_2O_3) A refractory material that increases the viscosity of a glaze, making it less runny, and that helps to control the melting point of a glaze. The main sources of alumina are china clay and ball clay. Because of its high melting point, only a small amount of alumina is needed—the proportion can be higher in a high-fire glaze. The quantity of alumina is increased for a matt surface and decreased if a crystalline glaze is desired. Alumina also helps make glazes more durable.

M amblygonite ($Li \cdot AIF \cdot PO_4$) A lithium ore that is an active flux; it also gives phosphoric opacity in glazes. Amblygonite is generally fired in an oxidation atmosphere; excessive amounts of it in a glaze may result in blistering. Spodumene and lepidolite can be used as a substitute for amblygonite.

H antimony oxide (Sb_2O_3) Infrequently used to produce light yellow.

H barium carbonate ($BaCO_3$) A source of barium oxide for glazes.

H barium oxide (BaO) A refractory, but in high-fire glazes it acts as a flux. Barium oxide helps produce a matt surface; it also adds brilliance to certain colors.

H bentonite ($Al_2O_3 \cdot 4SiO_2 \cdot 9H_2O$) A colloidal clay of volcanic origin that increases the plasticity of other clays. Bentonite is used in glazes to keep glaze particles in suspension. Its formula varies according to its source.

H **bismuth subnitrate** ($BiO \cdot NO_3 \cdot H_2O$)   In a diluted solution, commonly sprayed on red-hot raku glaze and then reduced to create a lustrous opalescent effect.

S **bone ash** ($Ca_3(PO_4)_2$) (**tricalcium phosphate**) Formulas vary. Made from animal bones, bone ash is source of calcium and phosphate, as well as a plasticizer for clay bodies. Used in clay bodies such as bone china, it lowers the clay's maturing point and increases its translucency. In glazes, it gives texture and acts as an opacifier.

M **borax** ($Na_2O \cdot 2B_2O_3 \cdot 1OH_2O$)   Generally used in fritted form, since it is soluble in water. Borax is a low-fire flux, but small amounts in high-fire glazes can help a glaze melt more smoothly. It is a source of sodium and boric oxides.

M **boric oxide** (B_2O_3) (**boron**)   A useful flux that operates at both high and low temperatures. It helps produce a smooth glaze and increases the brilliance of colors. Although a glass-forming material, boric oxide is also a strong flux at high temperatures. With iron, it may produce opalescent blues.

M **boron**   See **boric oxide.**

H **cadmium sulfide** (CdS)   Used with selenium in stains and low-fire frits for overglazes to produce red and orange. **It can be released into food, so do not use on food containers.**

S **calcium chloride** ($CaCl_2$)   Useful as a **flocculant** to keep glazes in suspension. A small amount of a diluted solution of calcium chloride is added to glazes to help keep compounds from settling.

N **calcium oxide** (CaO)   A useful glaze ingredient. Glazes with calcium are durable and resistant to acids. It has a high melting point but is a very active flux at high temperatures. For this reason, it is used especially in porcelain glazes. In low-fire glazes, it is usually combined with other fluxes. See also **whiting.**

china clay   See **kaolin.**

H **chromium oxide** (Cr_2O_3)   In glazes without zinc, it yields green; with zinc, it produces browns and tans. With tin, under proper conditions, it may produce pink. Reduction darkens the green color.

H **clay** (theoretical formula $Al_2O_3 \cdot 2SiO_2 \cdot 2H_2O$) Clay bodies are made up of various types of clays and range from low-fire to porcelain. In glazes, clay is generally used in the form of kaolin or ball clay to provide alumina and silica. Amounts will vary according to the particular clay used. In a glaze, it helps to keep the ingredients suspended and helps the glaze adhere to the ware.

M **cobalt oxide** (CoO) and **cobalt carbonate** ($CoCO_3$)   Formulas vary. These strong blue colorants do not burn out; used for decoration, cobalt can be fired from low to high temperatures. Cobalt alone gives rather strong blues that can be softened by adding manganese, iron, rutile, or nickel. A combination of cobalt oxide, chromium oxide, manganese oxide, and iron oxide produces a strong black.

M **colemanite** ($2CaO \cdot 3B_2O_3 \cdot 5H_2O$) (**calcium borate**)   A source of boric oxide in insoluble form, it also yields calcium oxide. Acting as a flux in both high- and low-fire glazes, it is also popular for the effects it produces in glazes—with rutile, for example, it gives a mottled appearance and may also give a milky blue. (See **gerstley borate.**)

M **copper oxide** (CuO) and **copper carbonate** ($CuCO_3$)   Copper gives greens, blues, or reds depending on the other ingredients in the glaze and the atmosphere in the kiln. In reduction copper produces reds in certain glazes; in oxidation it gives greens; and in alkaline glazes it gives turquoise. Copper was used in China to produce the famous ox-blood and peach-bloom glazes.

H **Cornish stone (Cornwall stone)** (theoretical formula $K_2O \cdot Al_2O_3 \cdot 8SiO_2$)   Formula varies; an English feldspathic material that requires high temperatures to fuse. It shrinks less than kaolin and feldspar, so it is less subject to glaze defects. It also helps form tough, hard glazes. Used as a source of silica, Cornish stone contains varying amounts of silica as well as potassium and sodium. In ancient China a similar rock called *petuntze* made possible the development of porcelain.

M **cryolite** (Na_3AlF_6)   A natural source of sodium. Cryolite can be used when both sodium and alumina are needed. It gives brilliant colors, but sometimes glazes containing it are subject to pits.

S **dolomite** ($CaCO_3 \cdot MgCO_3$)   A natural source of magnesium and calcium oxides. Used as a flux in stoneware glazes, it helps produce smooth matt surfaces and can help in crystal formation.

H **feldspar** (also spelled **felspar**)   Yields alumina and silica. Feldspars vary in composition and availability, with some containing potash and others containing soda. The formula of a commercial feldspar is usually available from the supplier, so you can see which oxides are present (see Chapter 1D). At high temperatures (e.g. 2280°F/1250°C), some feldspars melt with no additional flux. At lower temperatures, talc, dolomite, gerstley borate, or whiting is added to lower their melting point. Feldspar is used in porcelain clay bodies.

ferric oxide, ferrous oxide, and **ferro-ferric oxide**   See **iron.**

H **flint** (SiO_2) **(Quartz)**   The main source of silica in glazes; combines with a variety of fluxes to fuse at lower temperatures. In glazes it increases viscosity and hardness. In clay bodies, use coarser mesh (around 200); for glazes, use finer grind (around 300 mesh).

H **fluorspar** (CaF_2) **(calcium fluoride)**   Used in some glazes as a source of calcium; fluxes at a lower temperature than most calcium compounds. It helps develop the blue-greens of copper in oxidation firing. **Toxic fumes of fluorine gas are released in firing.**

M **gerstley borate** ($2CaO \cdot 3B_2O_3 \cdot 5H_2O$)   A source of boric oxide. Used as a flux, it is more stable than colemanite, another source of boric oxide. (See **colemanite.**)

N **ilmenite** ($FeO \cdot TiO_2$)   An ore in granular or powder form; contains both iron and titanium. Added to glazes, the granular form gives specks of dark color. It may also encourage crystals in glazes.

N **iron**   Varying amounts of iron are responsible for the buff and reddish colors of natural earthenware clays, where its fluxing action lowers their firing temperatures. Iron is also used in glazes to give warm cream or yellowish tones, tans, red-browns, and black; in reduction it gives grays, blue-greens, and black (see Chapter 1F). Its most commonly used forms are:

N **ferric oxide** (Fe_2O_3)   Red iron oxide or hematite

N **ferrous oxide** (FeO)   Black iron oxide

N **ferro-ferric oxide** (Fe_3O_4)   Magnetite

H **iron chromate** ($FeCrO_4$)   Usually gives grays and browns. With copper, it yields black; with tin it may give pink or red-brown.

H **kaolin** (theoretical formula $Al_2O_3 \cdot 2SiO_2 \cdot 2H_2O$) **(China clay)**   The main source of alumina and silica in glazes. Since it contains only traces of iron, it is also used in white clay bodies. (For example, EPK kaolin contains .42% iron; [English]. 60% iron, and Georgia .40% iron.)

H **lead oxide** (PbO)   A very active flux at low temperatures, used for this purpose for many centuries in the Near East, Europe, and the United

States until its toxicity was understood. When fritted with silica, the danger of handling this poisonous material is lessened, but even fritted lead is suspect. **We do not recommend the use of lead,** but if you do use a commercial lead frit in a glaze, fire it properly to avoid releasing lead into food, and check the frit to make sure there is enough silica in proportion to the lead—at least in the proportion of ($PbO \cdot 2SiO_2$). If in doubt, get a laboratory to test. **Red lead and white lead are highly toxic raw materials.**

M **lepidolite** ($LiF \cdot KF \cdot Al_2O_3 \cdot 3SiO_3$)   Formula varies; used in china bodies and as a flux in some high-fire glazes. It contains lithium and helps make most glazes brighter than soda or potash feldspars, but it can cause pitting.

lime   See **calcium oxide** and **whiting.**

M **lithium carbonate** (Li_2CO_3)   A source of lithium in glazes. At high temperatures it is an active flux, allowing the use of more alumina and silica in alkaline glazes to increase their hardness. It widens the firing range and brightens the colors, as well as having low expansion and contraction coefficients, helping the glaze fit.

H **macaloid**   A suspending agent in glazes similar in effect to bentonite. It is also a plasticizer in clay bodies.

N **magnesium carbonate** ($MgCO_3$)   Provides magnesium oxide. It is often introduced into glazes as a high-fire flux and matting agent.

N **magnesium oxide** (MgO)   Acts as a flux at high temperatures and a refractory in lower firings. It increases viscosity, improves the adhesion of glazes, and at high temperatures gives a smooth surface. At lower temperatures, it helps produce matt, opaque surfaces.

N **magnetite** (Fe_3O_4)   The mineral form of black iron oxide. It produces speckling in clays or glazes.

M **manganese carbonate** ($MnCO_3$)   A strong flux that produces light browns. In alkaline glazes it gives a purplish color.

H **manganese dioxide** (MnO_2)   A strong flux that gives purple when used with alkaline fluxes (sodium, potassium, and lithium) but usually brown in most glazes. Used with cobalt, depending on the other ingredients, purple or black may develop.

H **nepheline syenite** ($K_2O \cdot 3Na_2O \cdot 4Al_2O_3 \cdot 9SiO_2$)   A potash feldspar. Since it has more potassium and sodium, it melts at lower temperatures and is particularly useful in medium-range temperatures in both clays and glazes. It mutes the color of bright colorants in glazes. Its formula varies depending on its sources.

M nickel carbonate ($NiCO_3$)   Used as a colorant to produce muted browns, blues, grays, greens, and yellows.

M nickel oxide (NiO)   A refractory that will dull down other colors in a glaze. It produces muted colors such as browns, grays, and greens. When applied as a stain to bisque-fired porcelain and glaze-fired to cone 5, it yields a lime green.

S Opax   One of several commercial opacifiers. See **tin oxide.**

H pearl ash   See **potassium carbonate.**

H petalite ($Li_2O \cdot Al_2O_3 \cdot 8SiO_3$)   A lithium feldspar used in clay bodies and glazes to reduce thermal expansion.

H potassium carbonate (K_2CO_3)   Used in frits as a source of potassium. **This is a soluble material that is highly toxic in its raw state.**

H potassium dichromate ($K_2Cr_2O_7$)   Acts as a green colorant with boric acid. In a frit, with tin in low-fire glazes, it develops red and orange. **It is soluble and poisonous in its raw state.**

H potassium oxide (K_2O)   An active flux that operates at all temperatures. It has a high coefficient of thermal expansion that can cause crazing if used in large amounts. Potassium oxide is a component of feldspars and commercial frits.

M pyrophyllite ($Al_2O_3 \cdot 4SiO_2 \cdot H_2O$) (**aluminum silicate**)   By decreasing thermal expansion, shrinkage, and cracking, it extends the firing range of clay bodies.

H quartz   See **flint.**

N rutile (TiO_2) (**titanium dioxide**)   An ore that contains titanium and some iron. When fired in oxidation. It gives tans and browns, often in streaks. In reduction, it can give blues and oranges. In glazes with copper, cobalt, chrome, or iron, it may produce subtle gray colors. Rutile promotes the growth of crystals.

H Seattle slip   A slip glaze mined in Washington, offered as a substitute for Albany slip.

H Sheffield slip   A slip glaze mined in Massachusetts, offered as a substitute for Albany slip.

H silica (flint) (SiO_2)   The essential glass-forming oxide. It is the high silica content in high-fire glazes that causes them to be more durable and have greater resistance to chemicals, so the more silica used in a glaze the harder it will be. Silica requires high temperatures to fuse. At

lower temperatures it is necessary to bring down the melting point of silica with a flux. **Free silica dust is extremely damaging to the lungs.**

H silicon carbide (SiC)   In powder form, used in glazes to produce local reduction with copper oxide. In granular form it adds specks to glazes. It is a chief ingredient in heat-resistant kiln furniture.

H soda ash   See **sodium carbonate.**

H sodium carbonate (Na_2CO_3) (**soda ash**)   An active glaze flux, usually used only in frit form because it is soluble. It is also a deflocculant. When used in a clay body for slip casting, it reduces the amount of water needed.

M sodium oxide (Na_2O)   Used widely in low-fire glazes as a flux. It can also be used in high-fire glazes; when introduced into a kiln at at least 1940°F/1060°C, it will combine with the silica in clay to form a glaze. Sodium oxide has a high expansion coefficient that can cause crazing. Glazes high in sodium are apt to weather and flake off. It is most useful if used with other fluxes. **Fumes of sodium when released in salt glaze firing are caustic.**

M sodium silicate ($Na_2 \cdot SiO_2$)   Formula varies; used as a deflocculant in casting slips, where it helps keep the particles in suspension. It also increases fluidity, reducing the amount of water needed to form a slip, thus reducing shrinkage. Sodium silicate is also used in producing crystalline glazes.

M spinel   Natural spinels include **magnesium aluminate** ($MgO \cdot AL_2O_3$), and **beryllium aluminate** ($BeO \cdot Al_2O_3$).   Spinels are often synthetically produced and used to stabilize colorants in clays and glazes.

M spodumene ($Li_2O \cdot Al_2O_3 \cdot 4SiO_2$)   A source of lithium in glazes. If used instead of feldspar, it lowers the fusing temperature and helps to eliminate crazing.

H stannous chloride   In a diluted solution it is commonly sprayed on red-hot raku glaze and then reduced to create a lustrous mother-of-pearl effect. Or it is added to a glaze and then fired in a reducing atmosphere.

M strontium carbonate ($SrCO_3$)   A glaze flux with a wide firing range. It is also used in glazes to lessen crazing and improve the hardness of the fired glaze.

S Superpax ($ZrSiO_4$)   An opacifier that contains zirconium and produces a semiopaque white. It also helps control texture, crazing resistance, and color stability in glazes. See **tin oxide.**

H **talc** ($3MgO \cdot 4SiO_2 \cdot H_2O$) (**magnesium silicate**) Formula varies; used widely in low-fire clay bodies. It can also be used as an opacifier in glazes. As a source of magnesium, it acts as an effective high-fire glaze flux as well as lowering the melting temperatures of ball clays, feldspars, and kaolin in clay bodies. **Some talc contains asbestos, which is harmful to the lungs.** Non-asbestos talc is now available.

S **tin oxide** (SnO_2) Gives opaque and semiopaque white. It has been used for centuries to create opaque glazes to cover the reddish tones of earthenware. Since it is relatively expensive, many ceramists now use commercial products such as **Zircopax, Superpax,** and **Opax** to take its place.

S **titanium dioxide** (TiO_2) An opacifier that also helps create a somewhat matt surface. It produces white and cream opaque glazes. Titanium oxide is used in frit form or combined with other chemicals. (Rutile is a source of titanium that also contains iron.)

H **vanadium pentoxide** (V_2O_5) Alone, it gives light yellow; with tin, it gives a bright yellow. Reduced, it can produce blue-gray.

S **whiting** ($CaCO_3$) (**calcium carbonate**) The main source of calcium oxide in glazes and an important high-fire flux. Small amounts can be added to low-fire alkaline glazes to increase durability.

M **wollastonite** ($Ca \cdot SiO_3$) (**calcium silicate**) Used in clays and glazes as a source of calcium oxide; reduces shrinkage and increases strength. It is often introduced into clays and glazes for ware that may need to resist thermal shock, such as ovenware.

S **zinc oxide** (ZnO) A high-fire flux that reduces thermal expansion. It increases the strength of glazes and helps produce smooth surfaces. Zinc oxide is often used as a substitute for lead. In small amounts it helps create matt glazes; too much, however, causes glazes to become dry, to pit, or to crawl.

S **zirconium oxide** (ZrO_2) An opacifier, usually fritted with other oxides. It is not as strong as tin, but it is cheaper.

S **Zircopax** ($ZrSi_4$) A commercial zirconium opacifier, generally used where semiopaque glaze is desired. See **tin oxide.**

1F

Colorants and Opacifiers

 Many of these materials are toxic, and you must take precautions when using them. The relative toxicity is indicated by the following letters:

H = highly toxic   **S = slightly toxic**
M = moderately toxic   **N = nuisance**

In addition to these colorants, many glaze and clay body stains are available commercially. Check ceramic supply catalogues to see the range of colors.

Colorants	Colors Yielded	Percentage
H Antimony oxide Sb_2O_3	Below cones 1 or 2, infrequently used for light yellows.	10–20
H Cadmium sulfide CdS	In low-fire overglazes produces red, disappears if fired over cone 010. Usually combined with selenium in stain.	10–20
M Chromium oxide Cr_2O_3	Greens; with tin gives pinks; with zinc, produces browns. In reduction, may darken or blacken colors.	1–6
M Cobalt carbonate $CoCO_3$ **M Cobalt oxide** CoO	Blues; with magnesium, gives purple. Higher percentage gives blue-black. Powerful colorant, frequently used with iron, rutile, manganese, or nickel to soften harsh color. Withstands high firing. Carbonate with manganese, iron, or ochre gives black tones.	.01–2
M Copper carbonate $CuCO_3$ **M Copper oxide** CuO	Blue and turquoise in alkaline glazes. In lead glazes, gives soft greens **(copper facilitates release of toxic lead in contact with acidic foods)**. In some high-fire glazes, copper gives blues; in others, browns. In certain formulations and firing conditions, produces the ox-blood and peach-bloom glazes of ancient China.	1–5
Ilmenite $FeO \cdot TiO_2$	Gives brown specks and spots.	1–7

Colorants	Colors Yielded	Percentage
Iron **Ferric oxide** Fe_2O_3 (red) **Ferrous oxide** FeO **Ferro-ferric oxide** Fe_3O_4 H **Iron chromate** $FeCrO_4$	Can produce a wide range of colors in clay or glaze. In most glazes, from tans to reddish brown to black. With other oxides it modifies their brilliance. Under correct firing conditions produces the Japanese tenmoku or the famous gray-green celadon of China.	1–10
H **Manganese carbonate** $MnCO_3$ H **Manganese dioxide** MnO_2	In alkaline glazes, gives purples; with cobalt, produces violets. In high-fire reduction, produces brown; with cobalt, yields violets.	2–10
N **Nickel oxide** NiO	Browns and grays. Used mostly to modify other oxides. In some reduction glazes with zinc, it *may* yield yellows or blues, but results vary.	1–3
H **Potassium dichromate** (bichromate) $K_2Cr_2O_7$	Soluble, used in frit form. In low-fire glazes with boric oxide, gives greens; with tin, gives reds and oranges.	1–10
N **Rutile** TiO_2	Tans and browns. With cobalt, and sometimes with iron, gives blues and oranges. Produces streaks and mottled effects.	2–10
S **Tin oxide** SnO_2	In low-fire glazes, gives soft, opaque whites. Used as opacifier in early Persian, Spanish, and Italian tin glazes. Higher percentage gives opaque glaze; lower percentage yields semi-opaque glaze.	5–12
Titanium dioxide TiO_2	Whites and creams.	5–15
H **Vanadium oxide** (pentoxide) V_2O_5	Generally used in frit, with tin. Gives opaque yellows.	5–10

Opacifiers	Percentage
Tin oxide	5–12
Titanium dioxide	5–15
Zircopax	5–15
Superpax	5–15
Ultrox	5–15

Notes:

Tin oxide provides white when introduced into glazes in oxidation firing, or off-white in reduction firing. It also possesses strong opacifying properties; therefore, a smaller percentage is usually necessary when formulating a glaze. Since tin is substantially more expensive than the other opacifiers listed, Superpax and Zircopax are commonly used instead, or along with a smaller percentage of tin oxide. Titanium dioxide generally yields soft cream whites and may be combined with the other opacifiers to develop a range of white glazes.

2A

Bisque and Single Firing; Orton and Seger Cones; Converting Centigrade and Fahrenheit

BISQUE AND SINGLE FIRING

Kiln Temperature Rise per Hour Based on Cone 05 (1915°F/1046°C)

Use the following chart only as a guide in establishing firing patterns for ware. Differing clay types—such as a smooth-body porcelain or a heavily grogged stoneware—will have varying firing patterns even if the objects have the same thickness of walls. Coarse clays can generally be fired faster.

Kiln size and fuel difference will also affect temperature rise. In addition, different types of kiln brick, or a ceramic fiber interior, will affect the heat saturation of ware per hour of temperature rise. Variations in moisture content of the ware when it is placed in the kiln will also affect the temperature-rise-per-hour pattern. This chart is based on establishing a firing pattern in relation to the thickest portion of a work. The temperature ranges are *averages* based on the total number of hours required to fire the ware to cone 05.

Temperature Rise per Hour	Type and Thickness of Object to Be Fired
25–40°F/–6.4–4.4°C	¾–6 in. (19–152 mm) Massive sculpture or handbuilt
40–60°F/4.4–15.5°C	⅜–¾ in. (10–19 mm) Handbuilt, wheel-thrown
60–100°F/15.5–37.7°C	3/16–⅜ in. (5–10 mm) Small handbuilt, wheel-thrown
100–210°F/37.7–98.8°C	⅛–3/16 in. (3–5 mm) Slip-cast ware, thin wheel-thrown, thin handbuilt

ORTON AND SEGER CONES

Kiln Interior Colors; Comparative Temperatures (Centigrade and Fahrenheit); for Orton and Seger Cones (Large Cones, Rise of 270°F/150°C per Hour, *small cones, rise of 540°F/300°C per Hour); Maturing Points of Clays and Glazes

Kiln Interior	Seger Cone	Degrees C	Degrees F	Orton Cone	Clays	Glazes
Black		400	752			
		630	1166	022*	Clay dehydrates	Lusters
		643	1189	021*		
Dull red-orange		666	1231	020*		China paint (020–016)
		693	1279	019		
	019	685	1265			
	018	705	1301			
		732	1350	018		
	017	730	1346			
		761	1402	017		
	016	755	1391			
	015a	780	1436			
		794	1461	016		
		816	1501	015	Low-fire ware (015–1)	Low-fire glazes (015–1)
Red-orange		836	1537	014		Raku glazes (014–05)
		859	1578	013		
		880	1616	012		
		892	1638	011		
		913	1675	010	Bisque ware (010–05)	
		928	1702	09		
	09a	935	1715			
Orange	08a	954	1749	08		
	07a	970	1778			
		985	1805	07		
	06a	990	1803			
		1011	1852	06		
	05a	1000	1832			
	04a	1025	1847			
		1046	1915	05		
	03a	1055	1931			
		1070	1958	04		
	02a	1085	1955			
		1101	2014	03		
	01a	1105	2021			

Kiln Interior					Maturing Point	
	Seger Cone	Degrees C	Degrees F	Orton Cone	Clays	Glazes
Yellow		1120	2048	02		
	1a	1125	2057			
		1137	2079	01		
	2a	1150	2102			
		1154	2109	1		
		1162	2124	2	Stoneware (mid-range) (2–7)	Stoneware glazes (mid-range) (2–7)
		1168	2134	3		
	3a	1170	2138			
		1181	2158	4		
	4a	1195	2183			
		1205	2201	5		
	5a	1215	2219			
		1241	2266	6		
	6a	1255	2291	7		
	7	1260	2300			
		1269	2316	8		Salt glaze (8–11)
					Stoneware (8–12)	Stoneware glazes (8–12)
	8	1278	2332	9	Porcelain (9–13)	Porcelain glazes (9–13)
	9	1300	2372			
		1303	2377	10		
White		1312	2394	11		
	10	1320	2408			
		1324	2415	12		
	11	1340	2444			
		1346	2455	13		

CONVERTING FAHRENHEIT TO CENTIGRADE AND CENTIGRADE TO FAHRENHEIT

To convert Fahrenheit to centigrade (Celsius), subtract 32 degrees, multiply by 5, divide by 9.

To convert centigrade (Celsius) to Fahrenheit, multiply by 9, divide by 5, add 32 degrees.

2B

Kiln Firing Programs and Graphs

The following kiln firing programs and graphs are based on actual firings. The programs describe firings in electric or gas kilns of different styles and sizes using an oxidation or reduction atmosphere. The intention of the firing programs and graphs is to demonstrate the wide parameters of firing ware in a kiln. Each firing program details the total length of time to fire the ware, the temperature rise and decline per hour, the hold and soak patterns, the total hours per segment, and details on when to vent the kiln, open or close peepholes, open or lower a lid or close a door, ramp the temperature up or down or begin reducing the kiln.

Each firing scenario is set up for a different type of ware, clay, glaze, and firing temperature. By following these, you will learn that a china painted piece must be vented well and fired in 4 hours, that a handbuilt sculpture fires in 22 hours, that a crystalline glaze with three "hold/soak" segments fires in 18 hours, and that a 2- to 3-in. (50–76 mm) thick sculpture fires slowly over a period of 160 hours.

The firing programs, summarized in the following table, cover various cone firings: cone 018 (**1350**°F/732°C) for china paints, lusters, and metallics; cones 05–04 (**1915–1958**°F/1046–1070°C), bisque firings for slip-cast ware, handbuilt pottery, wheel-thrown pottery, sculpture of varying thicknesses; and cone 05 (**1915**°F/1046°C), cone 6 (**2266**°F/1241°C), and cone 10 (**2377**°F/1303°C) glaze firings. The programs and graphs are intended as study guides and can be adapted or adjusted to suit individual firing needs. For example, when the program notes for an electric-kiln firing to adjust a lid, door, or peephole; this instruction is reflective of American firing methods. In some countries, for safety reasons and by law, kilns are equipped with natural-draft or powered vents that expel the moisture and fumes from the kiln; and when the lid or door of an electric kiln is opened, the power automatically shuts off.

Summary of Chapter 2B Firing Programs

Ware Type	Firing Type	Total Hrs.
Wheel-thrown pottery or thin handbuilt sculpture, ³⁄₁₆–¼ in. (5–7 mm) thick	Bisque or glaze firing, cone 05 (**1915**°F/1046°C), oxidation	8 hrs.
Slip-cast pottery or sculpture, ³⁄₁₆–¼ in. (5–7 mm) thick	Bisque firing, cone 04 (**1958**°F/1070°C), oxidation	10 hrs.
Thick handbuilt sculpture or wheel-thrown pottery, ⅜ in. (10 mm) thick	Bisque firing, cone 05 (**1915**°F/1046°C), oxidation	22 hrs.
Thick tile, sculpture, or pottery, ½–⅝ in. (13–17 mm) thick	Bisque firing, cone 05 (**1915**°F/1046°C), oxidation	28.75 hrs.
Thick sculpture, pottery, or tile, 1 in. (25 mm) thick	Bisque firing, cone 05 (**1915**°F/1046°C), oxidation	66.4 hrs.
Thick wheel-thrown pottery, ¼ in. (7 mm) thick	Glaze firing, cone 6 (**2232**°F/1222°C), reduction	13.5 hrs.
Thick slip-cast or wheel-thrown pottery, ¼–⅜ in. (7–10 mm) thick	Crystalline glaze firing, cone 10 (**2377**°F/1303°C), oxidation	18 hrs.
Large-scale, thick handbuilt sculpture, 2–3 in. (51–76 mm) thick	Single firing, cone 10 (**2377**°F/1303°C), reduction	160 hrs.
Slip-cast porcelain pottery or sculpture, ³⁄₁₆ in. (5 mm) thick	China paint, luster, metallic overglaze firing, cone 018 (**1350**°F/732°C), oxidation	4 hrs.

Firing Program for Wheel-Thrown Pottery or Thin Handbuilt Sculpture, ³⁄₁₆–¼ in. (5–7 mm) Thick (8-Hour Firing)

Segment	Rate/hr.	Target Temp.	Hrs.	Hold hrs.	Notes
1	200°F/ 93°C	600°F/ 316°C	3	0	Prop the lid up 3 in. (76 mm) for 1 hour. Keep all peepholes open. Lower lid to 1 in. (25 mm) for 1 hour. Close the lid at **650°F/344°C**, and plug 75% of the peepholes
2	263°F/ 128°C	1915°F/ 1046°C	5	0	Fire with the top peephole open. Plug the peephole when the kiln turns off.

Firing Details: Bisque or Glaze Firing, Cone 05

Ware:	wheel-thrown pottery or thin handbuilt sculpture
Clay:	buff earthenware clay with 8% 20-mesh grog
Clay thickness:	³⁄₁₆–¼ in. (5–7 mm)
Kiln type:	top-loading, 3 cu. ft. (.08 cu. m), computerized
Fuel type:	electricity
Total firing time:	8 hours
Firing temperature:	Cone 05, **1915°F/1046°C**
Firing atmosphere:	oxidation
Firing speed:	medium-fast

Firing Graph for Wheel-Thrown Pottery or Thin Handbuilt Sculpture, ³⁄₁₆–¼ in. (5–7 mm) Thick (8-Hour Firing)

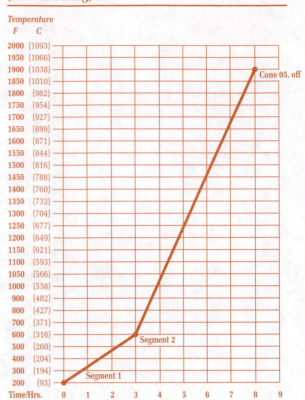

Firing Program for Slip-Cast Pottery or Sculpture, ³⁄₁₆–¼ in. (5–7 mm) Thick (10-Hour Firing)

Segment	Rate/hr.	Temp.	Hrs.	Hold hrs.	Notes
1	200°F/ 93°C	250°F/ 121°C	1.5	0	Prop the lid up 2 in. (51 mm). Keep all peep-holes open.
2	375°F/ 191°C	1000°F/ 538°C	2	0	Lower the lid to 1 in. (25mm) at 400°F/204°C.
3	100°F/ 38°C	1200°F/ 649°C	2	0	Close the lid at 600°F/316°C, and plug 50% of the peepholes.
4	300°F/ 149°C	1650°F/ 899°C	1.5	0	Close 75% of the peep-holes at 1000°F/538°C.
5	97°F/ 37°C	1940°F/ 1060°C	3	0	Fire with the top peep-hole open. Plug the peep-hole when kiln turns off.

Firing Details: Bisque Firing, Cone 04

Ware:	slip-cast pottery or sculpture
Clay:	smooth white earthenware casting body
Clay thickness:	³⁄₁₆–¼ in. (5–7 mm)
Kiln type:	top-loading, 15 cu. ft. (.42 cu. m), computerized
Fuel type:	electricity
Total firing time:	10 hours
Firing temperature:	Cone 04, 1958°F/1070°C
Firing atmosphere:	oxidation
Firing speed:	medium-fast

Firing Graph for Slip-cast Pottery or Sculpture, ³⁄₁₆–¼ in. (5–7 mm) Thick (10-Hour Firing)

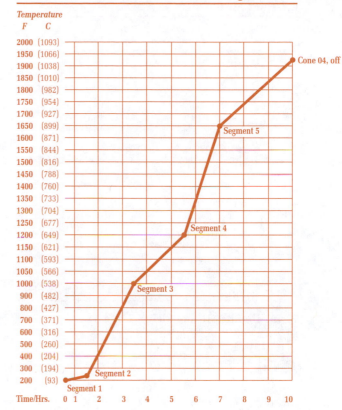

Firing Program for Thick Handbuilt Sculpture or Wheel-Thrown Pottery, ⅜ in. (10 mm) Thick (22-Hour Firing)

Segment	Rate/hr.	Temp.	Hrs.	Hold hrs.	Notes
1	60°F/ 16°C	240°F/ 116°C	4	0	Prop the lid up 3 in. (76 mm). Keep all peepholes open.
2	100°F/ 38°C	1040°F/ 561°C	8	0	Lower the lid to 1 in. (25 mm) at 400°F/204°C.
3	65°F/ 18°C	1300°F/ 1116°C	4	0	Close the lid at 600°F/316°C, and plug 50% of the peepholes.
4	133°F/ 56°C	1700°F/ 927°C	3	0	Close 75% of the peepholes at 1000°F/538°C.
5	72°F/ 22°C	1915°F/ 1046°C	3	0	Fire with the top peephole open. Plug the peephole when the kiln turns off.

Firing Details: Bisque Firing, Cone 05

Ware:	thick handbuilt sculpture or wheel-thrown pottery
Clay:	medium-coarse stoneware with 10% sand
Clay thickness:	⅜ in. (10 mm)
Kiln type:	top-loading, 7 cu. ft. (.19 cu. m), computerized
Fuel type:	electricity
Total firing time:	22 hours
Firing temperature:	Cone 05, 1915°F/1046°C
Firing atmosphere:	oxidation
Firing speed:	slow

Firing Graph for Thick Handbuilt Sculpture or Wheel-Thrown Pottery, ⅜ in. (10 mm) Thick (22-Hour Firing)

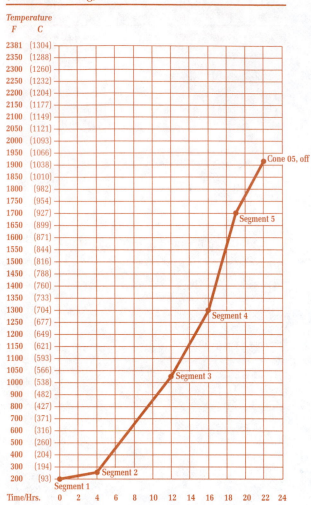

Firing Program for Thick Tile, Sculpture, or Pottery, ½–⅝ in. (13–17 mm) Thick (28.75-Hour Firing)

Segment	Rate/hr.	Temp.	Hrs.	Hold hrs.	Notes
1	40°F/ 4.4°C	240°F/ 648°C	6	0	Prop the lid up 4 in. (102 mm) for 6 hours. Keep all peepholes open.
2	60°F/ 16°C	1020°F/ 549°C	13	0	Lower the lid to 2 in. (51 mm) at 400°F/204°C. Close lid at 650°F/344°C.
3	80°F/ 27°C	1340°F/ 726°C	4	0	Plug 50% of the peepholes at 1000°F/538°C.
4	100°F/ 38°C	1915°F/ 1046°C	5.75	0	Fire with the top peephole open. Plug the peephole when the kiln turns off.

Firing Details: Bisque Firing, Cone 05

Ware:	thick tile, pottery, or sculpture
Clay:	red terra-cotta clay with 15% fine red grog
Clay thickness:	½–⅝ in. (13–17 mm)
Kiln type:	top-loading, 10 cu. ft. (.28 cu. m), computerized
Fuel type:	electricity
Total firing time:	28.75 hours
Firing temperature:	Cone 05, 1915°F/1046°C
Firing atmosphere:	oxidation
Firing speed:	slow

Firing Graph for Thick Tile, Sculpture, or Pottery, ½–⅝ in. (13–17 mm) Thick (28.75-Hour Firing)

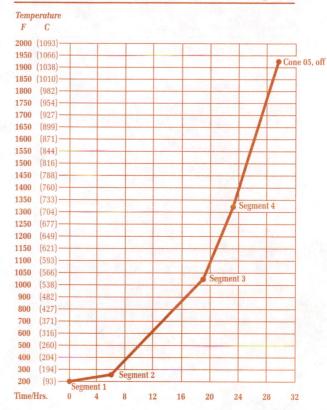

Firing Program for Thick Sculpture, Pottery, or Tile, 1 in. (25 mm) Thick (66.4-Hour Firing)

Segment	Rate/hr.	Temp.	Hrs.	Hold hrs.	Notes
1	30°F/ −1.1°C	180°F/ 79°C	6	12	Prop the lid up 4–8 in. (10–20 cm).* Keep all peepholes open. Close the lid after 8 to 12 hours.**
2	40°F/ 4.4°C	1015°F/ 546°C	21	5	
3	30°F/ −1.1°C	1345°F/ 729°C	11	0	Close 50% of the peep-holes at 1345°F/729°C.
4	50°F/ 10°C	1915°F/ 1046°C	11.4	0	At 1700°F/927°C close 75% of the peepholes, and leave 25% of the peepholes open.

Firing Details: Bisque or Single Glaze Firing, Cone 05

Ware:	thick handbuilt sculpture, pottery, or tiles
Clay:	stoneware with 4% paper pulp and 15% grog
Clay thickness:	1 in. (25 mm)
Kiln type:	top-loading oval kiln, 18 cu. ft. (.50 cu. m), computerized
Fuel type:	electricity
Total firing time:	66.4 hours
Firing temperature:	cone 05, 1915°F/1046°C
Firing atmosphere:	oxidation
Firing speed:	very slow

Notes: *Prop lid higher if ware is damp.
　　　　**Close lid sooner if newly loaded ware is dry.

Firing Graph for Thick Sculpture, Pottery, or Tile, 1 in. (25 mm) Thick (66.4-Hour Firing)

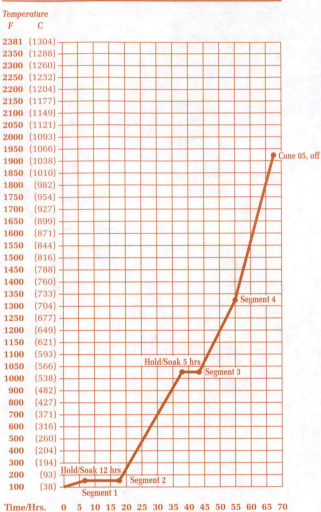

Gas Firing Program for Thick Wheel-Thrown Pottery, ¼–⅜ in. (7–10 mm) Thick (13.5-Hour Firing)

Segment	Rate/hr.	Temp.	Hrs.	Hold hrs.	Notes
1	200°F/ 93°C	400°F/ 204°C	2	0	Open the flue approximately halfway.
2	225°F/ 107°C	1125°F/ 607°C	5	0	Open the flue approximately one-quarter of the way.
3	185°F/ 85°C	2232°F/ 1224°C	6	.50	Open the flue approximately one-eighth of the way. Begin reduction at cone 08 until the end of the firing.

Firing Details: Glaze Firing, Cone 6

Ware:	thick wheel-thrown pottery
Clay:	medium-smooth white stoneware with 6% fine grog
Clay thickness:	¼–⅜ in. (7–10 mm)
Kiln type:	front-loading, 15 cu. ft. (.42 cu: m), downdraft
Fuel type:	propane or natural gas
Total firing time:	13.5 hours
Firing temperature:	2266°F/1241°C (approximately cone 6)
Hold/Soak:	30 minutes at 2266°F/1241°C
Firing atmosphere:	reduction
Firing speed:	medium

Firing Graph for Thick Wheel-Thrown Pottery, ¼–⅜ in. (7–10 mm) Thick (13.5-Hour Firing)

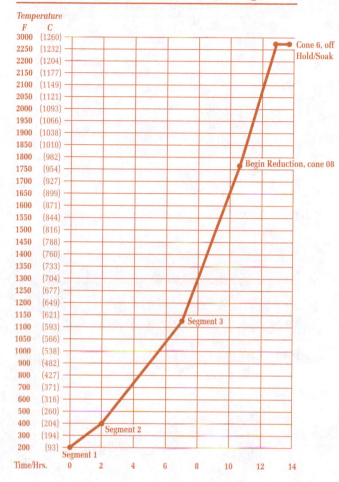

Firing Program for Thick Slip-Cast or Wheel-Thrown Pottery, ¼–⅜ in. (7–10 mm) Thick, with Crystalline Glaze (18-Hour Firing)

Segment	Rate/hr.	Temp.	Hrs.	Hold hrs.	Notes
1	200°F/ 93°C	1200°F/ 649°C	6	0	Open door ½–1 in. (13–25 mm). Keep all peepholes open. Close the shuttle door at 400°F/204°C.
2	250°F/ 121°C	1950°F/ 1066°C	3	0	
3	285°F/ 141°C	2377°F/ 1303°C	1.5	0	
4	254°F/ 124°C	2000°F/ 1093°C	1.5	3*	Close 75% of the peepholes.
5	50°F/ 10°C	1950°F/ 1066°C	.5	1*	Fire with the top peephole open.
6	72°F/ 22°C	1900°F/ 1038°C	.5	1*	Close the top peephole when the kiln turns off.

Firing Details: Glaze Firing, Cone 10

Ware:	thick slip-cast or wheel-thrown pottery
Clay:	porcelain
Clay thickness:	¼–⅜ in. (7–10 mm)
Glaze:	crystalline
Kiln type:	shuttle kiln, 20 cu. ft. (.56 cu. m), computerized
Fuel type:	electricity
Total firing time:	18 hours
Firing temperature:	Cone 10, 2377°F/1303°C
Firing atmosphere:	oxidation
Firing speed:	medium-slow

Note: *Hold/soak is critical to crystal growth.

Firing Graph for Thick Slip-cast or Wheel-Thrown Pottery, ¼–⅜ in. (7–10 mm) Thick, with Crystalline Glaze (18-Hour Firing)

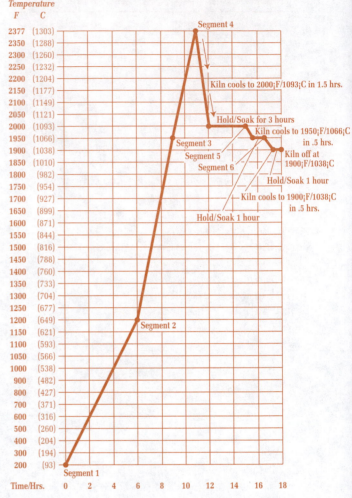

Gas Firing Program for Large-Scale Thick Handbuilt Sculpture, 2–3 in. (51–76 mm) Thick (160-Hour Firing)

Segment	Rate/hr.	Temp.	Hrs.	Hold hrs.	Notes
1	12°F/ −11°C	1200°F/ 649°C	100	0	**Day 1 to 4** Open the damper 100%.
2	15°F/ −9°C	1560°F/ 849°C	24	0	**Day 5** Keep the damper open 60–70%.
3	20°F/ −6.6°C	2040°F/ 1116°C	24	0	**Day 6** Keep the damper open 40%. At cone 05 (**1915°F/1046°C**) close the damper to 20–25% and begin reduction.
4	28°F/ −2.2°C	2377°F/ 1303°C	12	0	**Day 7** Keep the damper open 20–25%.

Firing Details: Single Firing, Cone 10

Ware:	large-scale, thick handbuilt sculpture
Clay:	coarse stoneware, with 20% grog
Clay thickness:	2–3 in. (51–76 mm)
Glaze:	stoneware
Kiln type:	updraft, 100 cu. ft. (2.83 cu. m.)
Fuel type:	natural gas
Total firing time:	160 hours
Firing temperature:	Cone 10, **2377°F/1303°C**
Firing atmosphere:	reduction (single firing)
Firing speed:	very slow

Firing Graph for Large-Scale, Thick Handbuilt Sculpture, 2–3 in. (51–76 mm) Thick (160-Hour Firing)

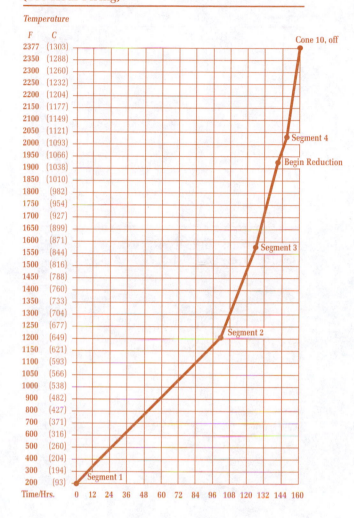

Firing Program for Slip-Cast Porcelain Pottery or Sculpture, ³⁄₁₆ in. (5 mm) Thick (4-Hour Firing)

Segment	Rate/hr.	Temp.	Hrs.	Hold hrs.	Notes
1	300°F/ 149°C	600°F/ 316°C	2	0	Prop the lid up 2 in. (51 mm) for 45 to 60 minutes.
					*Keep all of the peep-holes open throughout the entire firing. Lower the lid to 1 in. (25 mm) for 30 to 60 minutes. Close the lid at approxi-mately **600°F/316°C**.
2	375°F/ 183°C	1350°F/ 717°C	2	0	Fire with all of the peep-holes open. Option: Plug 75% of the peepholes when the kiln turns off.

Firing Details: China Paint, Luster, Metallic Overglaze Firing, Cone 018

Ware:	slip-cast porcelain pottery or sculpture
Clay:	translucent porcelain casting body
Clay thickness:	³⁄₁₆ in. (5 mm)
Kiln type:	top-loading, 3 cu. ft. (.08 cu. m), computerized
Fuel type:	electricity
Total firing time:	4 hours
Firing temperature:	Cone 018, **1350°F/732°C**
Firing atmosphere:	oxidation
Firing speed:	fast

Note: *Vent well throughout the entire firing.

Firing Graph for Slip-Cast Porcelain Pottery or Sculpture, ³⁄₁₆ in. (5 mm) Thick (4-Hour Firing)

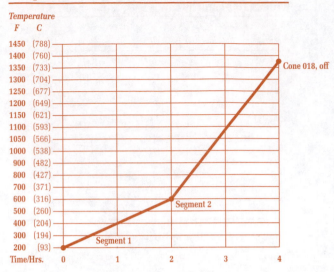

2C

Useful Measurements and Equivalents in U.S. and Metric Systems

American	U.S. Equivalent	Metric
Liquids		
1 fluid ounce		29.573 milliliters
1 fluid pint	16 fluid ounces	.473 liter
1 quart	2 fluid pints	.946 liter
1 gallon	4 fluid quarts	3.785 liters
4 quarts	1 gallon	3.785 liters
2.1134 pints		1 liter
1.0567 quarts		1 liter
0.26417 gallon		1 liter
Weight		
1 dram		1.772 grams
8 fluid drams	1 fluid ounce	29.573 milliliters
1 ounce		28.350 grams
1 pound	16 ounces	453.592 grams
2.2046 pounds		1,000 grams = 1 kilogram
35.274 ounces		1,000 grams = 1 kilogram
Length		
1 inch		2.54 centimeters
.3937 inch		1 centimeter
1 mil	.001 inch	.0254 millimeter
1 foot	12 inches	30.48 centimeter
1 yard	36 inches	.9144 meter
39.37 inches		1 meter
Volume		
1 cubic inch		16.38716 cubic centimeters
.0616234 cubic inch		1 cubic centimeter or .016387 liter
1 cubic foot	1,728 cubic inches	.028317 cubic meter
1 cubic yard	27 cubic feet	.76456 cubic meter
1.3079 cubic yards		1 cubic meter

3A

Changing the Flux in a Glaze

In the sample *Hands in Clay* tests given earlier, we changed only the colorants in some glazes. Colorants are not, of course, the only glaze components that can be changed and tested. Changing the amount of flux in a glaze, then running a series of tests on it, will prepare you for the testing you will do if you work through the example of calculating a glaze using chemical analysis in Chapter 3B.

The following tests alter the type and amount of flux in a cone 10 glaze, while the accompanying table shows a similar glaze formulated for low, medium, and high firings, allowing you to test those as well. (They are given for test purposes only.) If you test all three firing ranges, you will have a good idea of how fluxes work in a wide range of temperatures, as well as a good cross-reference between cone 05, cone 5, and cone 10 glazes. Although the cone 10 glaze is a reduction glaze, for test purposes you can use an electric kiln in oxidation—the results will just be different.

Components	Percentage		
	Cone 05	Cone 5	Cone 10
Potash feldspar (Custer)*			35.0
Nepheline syenite		45.0	
Calcium carbonate (whiting)		3.0	24.0
Frit 3195 (or 3811)	88.0		
Kaolin (Georgia)	10.0	13.0	28.0
Bentonite	2.0	2.0	
Silica 325 mesh (flint)			13.0
Gerstley borate		27.0	
PV clay		10.0	

*Custer feldspar is a potash feldspar.

In the following example, the formula is expressed in percentages, giving the option of mixing the batch in any amount. This means that the 35 parts of feldspar could be 35 grams, pounds, or tons, but the relationship remains the same. To get 500 g, you would multiply each number by 5, although actually you are multiplying each percentage by 500 to get the following:

Potash feldspar (Custer)	35% (.35)		175 g
Calcium carbonate (whiting)	24% (.24)	× 500	120 g
Kaolin (Georgia)	28% (.28)		140 g
Silica 325 mesh (flint)	13% (.13)		65 g
	100%		500 g

First mix the cone 10 glaze. Then add coloring materials in the following proportions. (If you wish to use another colorant, find the correct percentage in the chart in Chapter 1F):

Rutile	8% (.08)	× 500	40 g
Tin	1% (.01)		5 g

Dip a tile and mark it; then add 25 g (5%) of talc to a 500-g batch of glaze. In this instance, talc is used as a high-fire flux. Dip a tile in this mixture and mark it. Add another 25 g of talc, dip and mark another tile, and repeat the additions for 2 or 3 more tiles. Fire the test tiles at cone 10.

Repeat the same type of tests for the cone 5 and cone 05 glazes, adjusting their main fluxes by increasing or decreasing their percentages in the glazes. You can do this by altering the main flux (frit 3195 or 3811) in the cone 05 glaze and the Gerstley Borate in the cone 5 glaze. Increasing the fluxes will make your glazes more fluid in the kiln and glossier when fired, whereas decreasing the fluxes will make them less runny during firing and less shiny when fired to maturity.

3B
Calculating Glazes Using Chemical Analysis

For generations, potters developed glazes by experimentation. Based on the knowledge handed down from earlier potters, they tried out various combinations of materials much as you followed the progression of clay and glaze tests in Chapter 1. By working in this way, a ceramist can develop a clear sense of what each material does in combination with others without necessarily knowing the exact chemical composition of each material in the glaze. But if you want to go into the chemistry of glazes in greater depth, in this appendix you can follow a potter as he goes about analyzing, calculating, and testing a high-fire stoneware glaze. The method is the same whether the glaze is high-fire or low-fire, matt or glossy, transparent or opaque. By working through this step-by-step process, you will learn how to apply the basics of glaze calculation to any glaze.

Modern chemistry enables one to break down glaze materials into their chemical components and to work out formulas that represent the chemical, rather than the physical, proportions of its components. Using such chemical formulas, it is possible to analyze and compare glazes in a more detailed manner. The chemical structure, as well as the behavior of ceramic materials in the kiln, has now been analyzed, tested, observed, and recorded, and rules have been established to express their chemical relationships, making it easier for the ceramist to supply the needed chemical components of a glaze from the available ceramic materials. This method of calculation involves some

understanding of chemistry and of the basic atomic and molecular composition of glaze materials. A calculator and computer software (see Chapter 5B) make glaze calculation easier than it once was.

ELEMENTS AND COMPOUNDS

Before going further with the calculations, it is important to understand something about the chemical composition of the minerals used in glaze making. The earth's crust, from which these materials come, is made up of elements and compounds. An element is a substance that cannot be separated into substances different from itself by ordinary chemical means; it contains only one kind of atom. The atoms of the 114 known elements have been assigned weights in relation to the lightest element—hydrogen—which was given the weight of 1. In order to calculate glazes, you must use the atomic weights of the elements.

The elements, however, rarely exist in pure form but rather exist in compounds. Made up of combinations of different elements in a definite proportion, these compounds have been formed by natural forces and may exist as gases, liquids, or solids. The compounds with which the potter is mainly concerned are oxides produced when various elements become chemically combined with the oxygen that is so plentiful in our environment.

ATOMS AND MOLECULES

Molecules are the smallest particles of a compound that retain chemical identity with a substance in mass. The weight of a molecule consists of the total combined weights of all the atoms in that molecule. For example, water, which is made up of two atoms of hydrogen to one atom of oxygen, is written as H_2O. Since the atomic weight of one atom of hydrogen is 1, the weight of two atoms is 2. Add that 2 to the atomic weight of one atom of oxygen, which is 16, and you have a total molecular weight of 18. It is this concept of molecular weight that you will be concerned with in glaze calculation.

It helps to remember that the gram weight is the actual physical weight of the materials you will use when mixing a glaze, whereas the molecular weight is the chemical weight based on the atomic structure of the molecules. When making changes in a glaze, which is made up of different compounds, it is necessary to convert all calculations to molecular weights, since the weight of a compound in molecular terms differs markedly from its physical weight. If you simply mixed by gram weight, you would not achieve the desired result. Here we are concerned with the chemical reactions determined by the *proportion* of molecules of the various substances, rather than with the gross amounts of the substances.

EXAMPLE OF GLAZE CALCULATION

Now let's follow a potter Larry Murphy through a sample calculation.

I need to calculate a cone 10 glaze for the interior of casseroles and cups. I want a glaze that is glossy and either colorless or a very light gray or off-white. Most glazes that don't have glaze-coloring oxides (such as cobalt, iron, or copper oxide) added to them turn out to be clear or light gray. I will test a glaze without coloring oxides, fire it, and see what it looks like. Later I can add a colorant or an opacifier if I wish and test again. Experience has given me some basic knowledge as a starting point. I know, for instance, that most cone 10 glazes have ingredients, by weight, in the following very general proportions:*

---

*Murphy used Kingman feldspar, but the glaze has been recalculated to use Custer feldspar rather than the original Kingman feldspar, which is no longer available.

Feldspar (either soda or potash)	35–50%
Clay (china clay or ball clay)	5–20%
Additional flux for texture (whiting, colemanite, talc, dolomite, etc.)	15–30%
Silica 325 mesh (flint, or quartz)	5–25%

Each of these ingredients functions in one or more ways in a glaze:

Feldspar 35–50% This extremely useful and important material is present in most glazes. In high-fire glazes it is usually the main flux because feldspars have a relatively low melting point (around 2264°F/1240°C). Feldspar lowers the point at which the silica fuses and will also bring some additional silica and alumina to the glaze. Used with another flux, the fusing point can be lowered even more.

Clay (china clay or ball clay) 5–20% This is the main source of the refractory alumina in a glaze. China clay is white, so for my particular glaze I would use china clay rather than ball clay, which fires to a gray or cream. The clay, along with the feldspar, will generally supply all the alumina needed in a glaze. The sticky physical property of clay when added to a glaze helps to keep the glaze on the ware.

Additional flux 15–30% One of several high-fire fluxing materials can be used, such as talc, whiting, dolomite, or colemanite (Gerstley Borate). The additional flux may lower the melting point of the glaze by a cone or two, or even more if large quantities are added, and will also bring other oxides to the glaze. Talc, for instance, contains magnesia and silica, while colemanite yields calcium and boric oxide. When you use feldspar alone as a flux, the fired glaze surface is usually glassy. If additional fluxes are used, the surface of the fired glaze changes. Potters use terms like *buttery, satin,* or *soft matt* to describe these glaze surfaces.

Silica (flint) 5–25% Flint (also called *quartz*) is the main source of silica, the glass-forming oxide. It is best to use as much silica as possible in a high fire glaze in order to give a glaze the desired qualities of durability, hardness, and resistance to acids.

Using these proportions as a rough guide, I'll select those ingredients available to me, mix a glaze by gram weight, and test it.

These are the proportions I choose:

Custer feldspar—because it is the principal and most efficient flux material, used to lower the melting point of silica	45% (.45)

China clay—because it is the source of the refractory, and it is whiter than ball clay   15% (.15)

Talc—because in combination with the feldspar it acts as a stoneware flux that promotes highly glossy textures at cone 9 or 10, as well as being an opacifier   15% (.15)

Silica, a glass former, makes the glaze durable, hard, and resistant to acids.   25% (.25)
                                          ——
                                         100%

Since I want to have enough glaze to dip the tiles, I'll mix a batch of 500 g. To do this, I'll multiply the preceding proportions by 500, to get the following amounts in grams:

Feldspar	225 g
China clay	75 g
Talc	75 g
Silica 325 mesh (flint)	125 g
	500 g

Now I measure out these ingredients on my gram scale and add 17 oz. (503 ml) of water to form a soupy mixture (see *Hands in Clay,* Chapter 14). This mixture is the basic glaze. After mixing these ingredients, I dip some test tiles in the glaze and put them in the kiln with pottery I am ready to fire to cone 10.

After I have fired the kiln and looked at the test tiles, I can see that the glaze has some characteristics I want to change. I'm unhappy with its rather bland, glassy, and uninteresting texture. I feel it lacks the smooth, rich quality I like in a stoneware glaze, so I decide to make some alterations in the glaze ingredients.

Since the proportions of feldspar, china clay, and silica are constants in most stoneware glazes, I decide not to change them. This means I'll have to make my alterations in the additional flux, which in this case is talc. But in order to decide how much to change the proportions of the talc, I have to get involved in some chemistry. I'll have to examine the molecular makeup of the glaze, as well as take into consideration certain known limits of amounts of materials, altering the formula of the glaze accordingly. Before I do that, I'll explain some basic procedures that apply to glaze calculation.

Empirical Formula

For the purposes of glaze calculation, the materials used in a glaze are divided into three categories, according to their function in glazes. In Table 1, these categories are arranged in columns. The fluxes (both high- and low-fire) are listed under the heading RO/R_2O (also called **bases**); the refractory materials are listed under the heading R_2O_3 (also called **neutrals**); and the main glass former is listed under the heading RO_2 (also called **acid**). In this method of listing the ingredients, R represents the element and the O represents oxygen.

Notice that the oxides in the flux column (RO/R_2O) are all made up of one or two atoms of the element for each atom of oxygen (for example, MgO, PbO, Na_2O). Some of these fluxes, like lead, are effective only in low-fire glazes. The second column (R_2O_3) contains the oxides that make up

TABLE 1   Glaze Oxides

Flux	Refractory	Glass Former
RO/R₂O (Bases)	R₂O₃ (Neutrals)	RO₂ (Acid)
Oxides of:		
Lead, PbO*	Alumina, Al_2O_3	Silica, SiO_2
Sodium, Na_2O	Boric oxide, B_2O_3**	
Potassium, K_2O†		
Zinc, ZnO		
Calcium, CaO		
Magnesium, MgO		
Barium, BaO†		
Lithium, Li_2O		
Strontium, SrO		

*Highly toxic (see Chapter 1E for toxicity of ceramic materials).

**This is a neutral that can function as an acid or a base. It is an effective flux in both low- and high-fire glazes.

the refractory ingredients. Notice that these oxides are all formed in a ratio of two atoms of the element to three atoms of the oxygen. The third column, which contains the glass-forming agent (silica), is labeled RO_2 because the oxide in it consists of the element combined with two atoms of oxygen.

This arrangement of glaze materials in three columns is called the *empirical method,* and glaze formulas that list ingredients in the same three-column arrangement are called *empirical formulas.* Later, when we discuss the *unity formula* and *limit formulas,* we will see that the three-column (empirical) method of writing formulas provides a convenient format for checking the proper proportions of glaze ingredients.

ATOMIC AND MOLECULAR WEIGHT

As we have seen, because ceramic materials vary so widely in weight, in order to calculate the chemical composition of a glaze, you cannot merely take so many grams of that material or so many grams of this. If you did, you might get many more molecules of the heavier material than you wanted. Unless you know the weight of the molecules in each of the materials, you cannot select 1 or 20 or 500 or 10,000 molecules.

Each of the 108 known elements has been assigned an atomic weight in relation to hydrogen (see Chapter 3C). Since the atomic weight of hydrogen is 1 and oxygen 16, calcium 40, and silica 28, this means that the atomic weight of oxygen is 16 times the weight of hydrogen, while calcium is 40 times the weight of hydrogen, and silica is 28 times the weight of hydrogen. Unfortunately, ceramic materials are not conveniently made up of pure elements, but rather combinations of elements. In order to find the molecular weight of each material, I must first refer to its chemical symbol in Chapter 3D to see the kind and number of atoms that compose the material. For example, the symbol for silica (or flint) is SiO_2, and that, I know, means silica consists of 1 atom of silicon (Si) and 2 atoms of oxygen (O_2). By looking at Chapter 3C, I see that the atomic weight of silicon is 28 and the atomic weight of oxygen is 16. Doing some arithmetic, I can figure out the molecular weight of flint. To do this, I first multiply the atomic weight of silicon by 1 atom:

$$\text{Silicon: } 28 \times 1 = 28$$

Then I multiply the atomic weight of oxygen by 2 atoms:

$$\text{Oxygen: } 16 \times 2 = 32$$

Added together these come to 60, which gives me the weight of one molecule of silica (that is, the molecular weight of SiO_2). However, I don't have to go through this arithmetic each time, for the molecular weights are listed in Chapter 3D.

Equivalent Weights

You will notice that there is also a column of equivalent weights in Chapter 3D and that, for some of the materials, the equivalent weight is not the same as the molecular weight. The reason for this is that some materials are structured in such a way that they would yield more or less than one molecule of the desired oxide. In these cases, an altered, or equivalent, weight has been assigned to the material in order to introduce one molecule of the desired oxide into the glaze formula (and other oxides in proportion). In these cases, the equivalent weight should be used because it will yield precise quantities for the purposes of glaze calculation.

The Unity Formula

Before I do the necessary calculations to change my glaze, I must explain one more procedure. You have seen the reason for the empirical formula and the three-column arrangement, and also how to express the materials in molecular weights. However, in a formula based on the relationship between three groups of materials, there must always be one constant for the purpose of comparison. Remember, it is the *relative* amount of the materials that is important in formulating a glaze. So, arbitrarily, it has been decided that the RO/R_2O column will always represent 1—or *unity.* By accepting this, and by comparing this column to the other two columns, you will always understand the relationships of the materials in a glaze. Remember my glossy white glaze? Its original recipe was as follows:

Custer feldspar	45%
China clay	15%
Talc	15%
Silica (flint)	25%
	100%

In order to be able to work with molecules, I will divide these percentages of the materials by their molecular weights (or their equivalent weights). By consulting Chapter 3D and 3E, I see that the molecular weight of Custer feldspar is 694, that of china clay is 258, that of talc is 379, and that of silica is 60.

Now, taking each material in turn, I do the necessary arithmetic to find out the existing proportional amounts of the glaze ingredients:

Components	Molecular Proportions
Custer feldspar	$45 \div 694 = .065$
China clay	$15 \div 258 = .058$
Talc	$15 \div 379 = .039$
Silica (flint)	$25 \div 60 = .417$

Now I can consult Chapters 3D and 3E for the formula of each of my ingredients. I know which materials I am using and the molecular proportion of each one in this particular glaze. The formula for talc, for example, is $3MgO \cdot 4SiO_2 \cdot H_2O$, and I have already worked out that its molecular proportion in this glaze is .039. With this information, I can now construct a chart of my own glaze, which will give me a clear picture of its contents and the relationship of the parts to each other. I do this by multiplying the molecular proportion of each raw material by the quantity of each oxide in its formula. For example, in the case of talc, which has 3 parts of magnesium, I multiply 3 by .039. This shows me that the talc will contribute .117 part of magnesium oxide to this glaze ($3 \times .039 = .117$).

There is one complication. Feldspars are composed of many oxides, so I must be sure to have the correct formula for the type of feldspar I use. Ceramic material suppliers usually provide the necessary information about the composition of various feldspars, but these formulas may vary somewhat depending on where the feldspar is mined. Also, feldspars usually have to be brought to unity. I have worked out the empirical formula for Custer feldspar:

RO/R_2O	R_2O_3	RO_2
CaO, .030	Al_2O_3, 1.04	SiO_2, 6.94
K_2O, .670		
Na_2O, .300		
FeO_2, trace*		

*Small amounts can be ignored.

This means that there is .300 part of sodium oxide, .670 part of potassium oxide, and .030 part of calcium oxide in the Custer feldspar formula, as well as 1.04 parts of alumina and 6.94 parts of silica.

Now I draw up a table in which I arrange the ingredients down the left side, next to the molecular proportions for my particular glaze (Table 2). Across the top I list the oxides that my materials will yield. This table makes it possible for me to see very clearly the quantity of each oxide that is present in my white glaze. Since water and gases burn away or change in the firing, they are not included in the calculations, nor are the small amounts of other elements in the feldspar.

Now, again using the three columns, I arrange my oxides according to the empirical formula:

RO/R_2O	R_2O_3	RO_2
CaO .002	Al_2O_3 .126	SiO_2 1.139
MgO .117		
K_2O .044		
Na_2O .020		
Totals .183	.126	1.139

As I said before, I want to make a unity formula by expressing the RO/R_2O column as a unit of 1. Now

TABLE 2

Material	Molecular Proportions	Oxides					
		SiO_2	Al_2O_3	CaO	MgO	K_2O	Na_2O
Custer feldspar	.065	.45	.068	.002		.044	.020
China clay	.058	.116	.058				
Talc	.039	.156			.117		
Silica (flint)	.417	.417					
Totals		1.139	.126	.002	.117	.044	.020

it adds up to .183. How do I fix this? By dividing everything in the preceding formula by .183, I get a true unity formula, as follows:

RO/R$_2$O		R$_2$O$_3$		RO$_2$	
CaO	.011	Al$_2$O$_3$	.688	SiO$_2$	6.224
MgO	.639				
K$_2$O	.241				
Na$_2$O	.109/.108				
Totals	1.00		.688		6.224

Limit Formulas

Now I can see my glaze expressed in a unity formula that can easily be analyzed and compared to other glazes. The amount of each oxide in the glaze can also be checked easily against the limits suggested below. These limit formulas have been worked out as guides to show the amount of each oxide that occurs in a particular type of glaze maturing at a particular temperature range. Remember, however, that although limit formulas are generally accurate, there are many glazes that exceed either the upper or lower limits but which can still be successful glazes. These limits should be taken only as broad guidelines and should not keep you from experimenting. However, in order to solve my problems with this particular glaze, it will help me to look at the proportions of the materials in the unity formula of my glaze and compare them to the limits suggested in the limit formula for stoneware or pocelain glazes in the cones 8–12 range.

Cones 8–12 Stoneware Limit Formula

KNaO	.2–.40	Al$_2$O$_3$	.3–.5	SiO$_2$	3.0–5.0
CaO	.4–.70	B$_2$O$_3$	.1–.3		
MgO	0–.35				
ZnO	0–.30				
BaO*	0–.30				

*Highly toxic

When I look at the two sets of numbers and compare the formula of my glaze with the limit formula, several facts become apparent:

1. My sodium and potassium are within limits. I combine these two ingredients by addition to get the total of the KNaO:

K$_2$O	.241
Na$_2$O	.109/.108
	.350 versus a limit of .2–.4

2. My magnesium is very high: .639 versus a limit of .35.
3. My alumina is high: .688 versus a limit of .5.
4. My silica is high: 6.224 versus a limit of 5.0.

So now I can figure out that the combination of high silica and high flux made a very shiny, glassy glaze, but it did not run off the test tile because the alumina was also high.

ANALYZING THE GLAZE

I now examine the glaze ingredients closely in view of their functions. This will give me some information about how to change the glaze so that it may suit my purposes better. After firing, I saw that the glaze was glossy. This means that despite the silica being high, the actual proportion of glass (silica) to glass melters (feldspar and talc) was all right. If there had been too much silica and not enough flux, the final product would have been underfired, rough, and granular. On the other hand, if there had been too much flux, the glaze would have run down off the wall of the test tile into a pool at the base of the tile. Also, I see that the glaze is not brittle, nor is it crazing, crackling, or shivering off the clay body. This means that the proportion of the refractory (alumina) must be all right. Too little alumina would cause the glaze to be brittle and probably shiver, whereas if there were too much alumina, the glaze surface would be matt and dull.

The only thing I find wrong with this glaze for my purposes is that I don't care for the texture. I know that texture is controlled largely by the oxides in the optional fluxes (such as calcium, magnesium, zinc, or barium). So, considering the high proportion of magnesium (.639 versus a limit of .35), I decide to reduce the magnesium to bring it within the usual limits. I'll then substitute another flux for the quantity of magnesium I remove. (Remember that I am still testing, and all experimentation at this point can be modified according to the results that show after the tiles have been fired in the kiln.)

I decide to reduce the magnesium by .30 to a total of .339 and to substitute .311 molecule of calcium. I choose calcium for several reasons: It is easily available in whiting, a staple in most pottery studios; it is known to provide a smooth, matt surface in some glazes; and it is a proven trouble-free stoneware flux. Also, when calcium is added in the form of whiting, it will promote a light color in the glaze, suiting my purpose.

After I have made the substitution, my formula looks like this:

K_2O .241 Al_2O_3 .688 SiO_2 6.224
Na_2O .109
MgO .339
CaO .311

Converting from Empirical Formula to Batch Recipe

Now that I have decided how to alter my empirical formula to achieve the desired results, I must find a way to supply the ingredients from the dry materials. I do this by constructing another table with the ceramic materials and their formulas on the left and the oxides of my empirical formula running across the top (Table 3). Starting with the oxides that come from single-oxide materials, I continue with the materials that have two or more oxides, putting the silica last. Under each oxide I enter the desired proportional amount needed as I determined them for my altered formula. Table 3 includes remarks to clarify the process for the reader.

To determine the required amounts of each material, I must fill in the table using the amounts I found in my empirical formula and which I have listed across the top of the table. Starting with the oxides that come from the materials that have only one oxide in them, I determine the required amounts by using the following equation:

$$\text{Proportional requirements of materials} = \frac{\text{Amount wanted in formula}}{\text{Amount present in material}}$$

For example, I want .3 CaO. Whiting has one part CaO, so I divide .3 by 1, which of course gives me .3. (If there were any other elements in whiting, I would have to multiply each of them by .3, since that is how much I will use of the entire material.) As you can see, my needs for CaO are thus satisfied entirely by the whiting. I can now go on to calculate the proportional figures for the remaining materials.

I need .339 MgO and I find that talc has 3 MgO in its formula. Therefore, I divide .339 by 3 to arrive at the proportional figure of .113 for talc. I then multiply each oxide in the talc formula by .113, which gives me .339 of MgO (satisfying my needs) and .452 of SiO_2. I subtract that amount of SiO_2 from my needed amount of 6.224 and put the remaining needed amount (5.772) in parentheses.

The next material listed in my empirical formula at the top of the chart is Na_2O, and I need .108/.109 part of it. In the Custer feldspar formula I see that there is .30 available. To get my proportional figure, I divide .108/.109 by .30 and get .361. I then multiply each part in the feldspar formula by .361 to get the equivalent amount of each part

contained in my empirical formula. So I get .109 Na_2O (satisfying the amount needed), .241 K_2O (also satisfying that amount needed), .375 Al_2O_3, which I subtract from the needed amount of .688, and I put the remaining amount needed (.313) in parentheses. Finally I get 2.505 SiO_2 and subtract that from the needed amount of 5.772 and put the remainder (3.267) in parentheses.

Now I have satisfied all my needs except for the remaining amounts of Al_2O_3 and SiO_2. I can complete my alumina needs with china clay by using .313 of it, since it contains one part of Al_2O_3. However, there are two parts of SiO_2 in china clay, and when I multiply by .313, I get .626. I subtract this amount from the needed 3.267, leaving me with 2.641 parts of silica still needed. I complete my remaining requirements by adding the needed amount (2.641) with flint, which is a nearly pure form of silica.

Now that I have determined the proportions required of each material, I simply multiply this amount by the molecular (or equivalent) weights for each ingredient. The molecular or equivalent weights of the most common materials are listed in Chapter 3D. The final result is shown in Table 4. A batch recipe is what I started with, and now I have another batch recipe of the altered glaze ready to mix, test, and fire.

Once again I will mix a batch of 500 g of the glaze, dip some test tiles in the batch, and fire them to cone 10. It is a good idea to dip several tiles and place them in different locations in the kiln to see if small variations in kiln atmosphere will affect the glaze.

The fired result of the test is a glaze that has changed somewhat. Its glossy finish has a softer texture that suits my purpose as a liner glaze. If I decide to alter it later, I could add a little Zircopax (2–10%) to try to introduce some opacity and whiteness to the glaze, or I could add some other colorants.

What I have followed here is the basic method for testing glazes using chemical analysis, using most of the procedures required in order to go from batch recipe to molecular formula and back to batch again. If you have followed this example through these procedures, you now have seen the basic process of calculating and analyzing glazes.

As you proceed to work with more complex materials and to formulate more sophisticated and elaborate glazes, the calculations can become more complex. However, no amount of knowledge of chemistry can substitute for patient testing and retesting of trial formulas in your own kiln, with your own clay body, and with the available materials. The use of chemistry answers many technical questions and gives you a method of formulating a glaze, but experience, patience, hard work, and aesthetic sensitivity are what really create beautiful glazes.

TABLE 3   From Empirical Formula to Batch Recipe

Material	Proportional Requirement	Remarks	CaO .311	MgO .339	Na_2O .108/.109	K_2O .241	Al_2O_3 .688	SiO_2 6.224
Whiting, $CaCO_3$	.311	I need .3 part of CaO. Whiting has 1 part CaO, so I divide .3 by 1 to get my proportional requirement.	Satisfied by $1 \times .3 = .3$ (still need .011)					
Talc, $3 MgO \cdot 4 SiO_2$	.113	I need .339 MgO. Talc has 3 MgO. The materials proportion is thus .339 ÷ 3 = .113. I multiply each part in talc by this figure. Magnesium is satisfied, but I need more silica.		Satisfied by $3 \times .113 = .339$				$4 \times .113 = .452$ (still need 5.772)
Custer feldspar, $.30 Na_2O \cdot .67 K_2O \cdot .03 CaO\ 1.04 Al_2O_3 \cdot 6.94 SiO_2$	.361	I need .108/.109 Na_2O. There is .30 Na_2O available in the feldspar. I divide .108 by .30 to get .361. Then I multiply each part in the feldspar formula by this figure. I find I still need more Al_2O_3 and SiO_2.	Satisfied by $.03 \times .361 = .011$		Satisfied by $.30 \times .361 = .108$	$.67 \times .361 = .241$	$1.04 \times .361 = .375$ (still need .313)	$6.94 \times .361 = 2.505$ (still need 3.267)
China clay, $Al_2O_3 \cdot 2 SiO_2$	.313	.313 Al_2O_3 is needed. There is one part Al_2O_3 available in china clay. .313 ÷ 1 = .313, which is the materials proportion still needed of alumina. China clay satisfies .626 silica. I still need 2.641 silica.					Satisfied by $1 \times .313 = .313$	$2 \times .305 = 610$ (still need 2.355)
Silica (flint), SiO_2	2.641	Remaining silica needed satisfied by 2.641 of flint.						Satisfied by $1 \times 2.641 = 2.641$

TABLE 4

Material	Proportional Amount	×	Molecular Weight (or Equivalent Weight)	=	Batch Amount (g)	Percentage
Whiting	0.311	×	100	=	31.1	6
Talc	0.113	×	378	=	42.7	8
Feldspar	0.361	×	694	=	250.5	44
China clay	0.313	×	258	=	80.8	14
Silica (flint)	2.641	×	60	=	158.5	28
					563.6 g	100%

3C

Atomic Weights of Elements Used in Ceramics

Element	Symbol	Atomic Weight	Element	Symbol	Atomic Weight
Aluminum	Al	26.98	Manganese	Ma	54.93
Antimony	Sb	121.75	Nickel	Ni	58.71
Barium	Ba	137.34	Nitrogen	N	14.00
Bismuth	Bi	208.98	Oxygen	O	15.99
Boron	B	10.81	Phosphorus	P	30.97
Cadmium	Cd	112.40	Platinum	Pt	195.09
Calcium	Ca	40.08	Potassium	K	39.10
Carbon	C	12.01	Selenium	Se	78.96
Chlorine	Cl	35.45	Silicon	Si	28.08
Chromium	Cr	51.99	Silver	Ag	107.86
Cobalt	Co	58.93	Sodium	Na	22.98
Copper	Cu	63.54	Strontium	Sr	87.62
Fluorine	F	18.99	Sulphur	S	32.06
Gold	Au	196.96	Tin	Sn	118.69
Hydrogen	H	1.00	Titanium	Ti	47.90
Iridium	Ir	192.22	Uranium	U	238.02
Iron	Fe	55.84	Vanadium	V	50.94
Lead	Pb	207.20	Zinc	Zn	65.37
Lithium	Li	6.94	Zirconium	Zr	91.22
Magnesium	Mg	24.30			

3D

Molecular and Equivalent Weights

Material	Formula	Molecular Weight	Equivalent Weight
Alumina	Al_2O_3	101.9	101.9
Antimony oxide	Sb_2O_3	291.5	291.5
Barium carbonate	$BaCO_3$	197.4	197.4
Barium oxide	BaO	153.4	153.4
Bone ash	$Ca_3(PO_4)_2$	310.3	103.0
Borax	$Na_2O \cdot 2B_2O_3 \cdot 10H_2O$	381.4	381.4
Boric acid (Boron)	$B_2O_3 \cdot 3H_2O$	123.7	123.7
Boric oxide	B_2O_3	69.6	69.6
Calcium borate (colemanite)	$2CaO \cdot 3B_2O_3 \cdot 5H_2O$	412.0	206.0
Calcium carbonate (whiting)	$CaCO_3$	100.09	100.1
China clay (kaolin)	$Al_2O_3 \cdot 2SiO_2 \cdot 2H_2O$	258.1	258.1
Chromium oxide	Cr_2O_3	152.0	152.0
Cobalt carbonate	$CoCO_3$	118.9	118.9
Cobalt oxide	CoO	74.9	74.9
Copper carbonate	$CuCO_3$	187.0	187.0
Copper oxide (cupric)	CuO	79.57	79.57
Copper oxide (cuprous)	Cu_2O	143.0	80.0
Cornish stone	$\begin{matrix} CaO \cdot 304 \\ Na_2O \cdot 340 \\ K_2O \cdot 356 \end{matrix} \begin{Bmatrix} Al_2O_3 \\ 1.075 \end{Bmatrix} \begin{matrix} SiO_2 \\ 8.10 \end{matrix}$	667.0	667.0
Cryolite (soda)	Na_3AlF_6	210.0	420.0
Dolomite	$CaCO_3 \cdot MgCO_3$	184.4	184.4
*Feldspar (lime)	$CaO \cdot Al_2O_3 \cdot 2SiO_2$	278.6	
*Feldspar (potash)	$K_2O \cdot Al_2O_3 \cdot 6SiO_2$	556.8	556.8
*Feldspar (soda)	$Na_2O \cdot Al_2O_3 \cdot 6SiO_2$	524.5	524.5
Flint	SiO_2	60.06	60.06
Ilmenite	$FeO \cdot TiO_2$	151.74	151.74
Iron chromate (ferrous-ferric)	$FeCrO_4$	172.0	172.0
Iron oxide, black (ferrous)	FeO	71.8	71.8
Iron oxide, red (ferric)	Fe_2O_3	159.7	159.7
Kaolin (calcined)	$Al_2O_3 \cdot 2SiO_2$	222.0	222.0

*Feldspar formulas vary. See Chapter 3E.

Material	Formula	Molecular Weight	Equivalent Weight
Lead carbonate (white lead)	$2PbCO_3 \cdot Pb(OH)_2$	775.6	223.0
Lead oxide	PbO	223.2	223.2
Lead oxide (red)	Pb_3O_4	685.6	228.0
Lithium carbonate	Li_2CO_3	73.9	73.9
Magnesium carbonate	$MgCO_3$	84.3	84.3
Magnesium oxide	MgO	40.3	40.3
Manganese carbonate	$MnCO_3$	114.9	114.9
Manganese dioxide	MnO_2	86.9	86.9
Nepheline syenite	$\begin{Bmatrix} K_2O \cdot 25 \\ Na_2O \cdot 75 \end{Bmatrix} \begin{Bmatrix} Al_2O_3 \\ 1 \cdot 11 \end{Bmatrix} \begin{matrix} SiO_2 \\ 4 \cdot 65 \end{matrix}$	462.0	462.0
Nickel oxide	NiO	74.7	74.7
Potassium carbonate (pearl ash)	K_2CO_3	138.2	138.2
Quartz (silica)	SiO_2	60.0	60.0
Rutile	TiO_2	79.1	79.1
Silica (flint)	SiO_2	60.1	60.1
Sodium carbonate (soda ash)	Na_2CO_3	106.0	106.0
Sodium silicate	$Na_2 \cdot SiO_3$	122.1	122.1
Spodumene	$Li_2O \cdot Al_2O_3 \cdot 4SiO_2$	372.2	372.2
Talc (magnesium silicate)	$3MgO \cdot 4SiO_2 \cdot H_2O$	378.96	378.96
Tin oxide	SnO_2	150.7	150.7
Titanium oxide	TiO_2	80.1	80.1
Vanadium pentoxide	V_2O_5	181.9	181.9
Whiting	$CaCO_3$	100.1	100.1
Wollastonite	$Ca \cdot SiO_3$	116.0	116.0
Zinc oxide	ZnO	81.4	81.4
Zirconium oxide	ZrO_2	123.2	123.2
Zirconium silicate (zircopax)	$ZrO_2 \cdot SiO_2$	182.9	182.9

3E

Formulas of Some Feldspars

The formulas and molecular weights may vary slightly depending on where the feldspar is mined and other factors.

Feldspar	Formula	Molecular Weight
Cornwall stone	.356 K_2O · 1.075 Al_2O_3 · 8.10 SiO_2 .340 Na_2O .304 CaO	667
Custer	.67 K_2O · 1.04 Al_2O_3 · 6.94 SiO_2 .30 Na_2O .03 CaO	694
Kona F-4 (56)	.58 NaO · 1.00 Al_2O_3 · 5.79 SiO_2 .26 K_2O .16 CaO	518
Lepidolite	.39 K_2O · 1.00 Al_2O_3 · 3.74 SiO_2 .06 Na_2O .55 Li_2O	383
Nepheline syenite	.75 Na_2O · 1.11 Al_2O_3 · 4.65 SiO_2 .25 K_2O	462
Oxford	.58 K_2O · 11.07 Al_2O_3 · 1.07 SiO_2 .42 Na_2O	556
Petalite	1.00 Li_2O · 1.00 Al_2O_3 · 8.00 SiO_2	612
Plastic vitrox	.61 K_2O · 1.33 Al_2O_3 · 14.00 SiO_2 .34 Na_2 .05 CaO	1051
Spodumene	1.00 Li_2O · 1.00 Al_2O_3 · 4.00 SiO_2	372
Volcanic ash	.47 KNaO · 1.09 Al_2O_3 · 9.52 SiO_2 .17 CaO .25 MgO .11 FeO	720

4A

Types of Plasters and Their Uses

Since plaster is an important material, if you wish to make multiples by casting with pots or sculpture, this chapter will provide you with useful information for making molds.

Plaster Type	Parts Water per 100 lb. (45.4 kg) Plaster	Setting Time	Density	Uses	Notes
Casting	67–80	20–25 min.[†]	soft	a, b, c, d, h, k	All-purpose; harder, somewhat coarser than Pottery Plaster #1
Pottery Plaster #1	67–70	20–25 min.[†]	softer	a, b, c, g	Used for slip-casting; excellent detail, produces high-quality casting molds[‡]
Hydrocal (white) TM*	38–42	20–30 min.[†]	hard	d, e	Used for sculpting and carving
Hydrocal A-11 TM*	42–44	16–20 min.[†]	hard	f, h, j	Original model-making
Hydrostone TM*	28–32	17–20 min.[†]	hardest	d, e, h, i	One of the hardest gypsum cements; used for molds, casting, finished art works
Ultracal 30 TM*	35–38	25–30 min.[†]	hard	f, h, j	Super strength gypsum cement; often used for original model-making, block and case, and mother molds

Letter Codes in "Uses" column:

a. Plaster bats, wedging table tops
b. Press molds
c. Slip-casting molds
d. Sculpting and carving
e. Casting art works
f. Model-making, block and case, and mother molds

g. Molds for jiggering
h. Cases for supporting flexible molds
i. RAM press dies
j. Template models
k. Waste molds

*Trademarks owned by United States Gypsum Company.

[†]Time varies according to age of material, temperature of water and atmospheric conditions, ratio of water to material, quantity of batch, and mixing methods.

[‡]Density will be affected by water-to-material ratio and mixing methods.

Soft = Can be easily sanded, chiseled, carved, and drilled.

Softer = Fine grain can be easily sanded, scraped with a metal rib, chiseled, carved, and drilled.

Hard = Can be filed, drilled, chiseled, and sanded.

Hardest = Can be filed, chiseled, and drilled.

4B

Common Plaster and Slip-Casting Problems and Solutions

The following lists identify common problems that arise in plaster mixing, mold-making, and slip-casting. They will help you understand the probable causes of and possible solutions to many of the difficulties you may encounter.

Plaster Problem	*Probable Cause and Solution*
1. *Plaster mold cracked while setting*	The plaster was undermixed. Mix the plaster solution more thoroughly before pouring.
2. *Plaster is still mushy after 1 hour*	Too much water was added to the plaster, so it will never set. Start again.
3. *Plaster set up while mixing*	The plaster was old. Start over, and use fresh plaster. *Or,* the water was too hot, and it accelerated the setting. *Or,* a contaminated bucket filled with plaster chip residue or other contaminants accelerated the set-up time.
4. *Ran out of plaster halfway through the pour*	Immediately mix and pour a new batch of plaster on top of the first batch. *Or,* if the first batch is still soft, wait until the plaster has set and has cooled down. Score the plaster heavily with deep lines with a nail or carving tool, then completely saturate the plaster for 5 minutes. Mix a new batch of plaster and pour it on top of the first batch.
5. *Plaster mold section or piece broke*	To reattach a section, dry the mold thoroughly. Apply a small amount of white glue to the broken pieces, being careful not to let any glue run into the face of the mold where the slip touches. Let the mended mold dry thoroughly before using.
6. *After casting a plaster section, there were pits or small air-pocket holes*	To patch pits or holes, saturate the section in water for about 5 minutes. Mix a small amount of plaster with the ratio of 2.75 parts plaster to 2 parts water. Let the mixture set up until creamy; then, with a spatula, carefully fill the holes and trim off any extra.
7. *Plaster mold interior surface has a crusty residue or scum*	Too much separating soap was painted on the original object or plaster section. Apply less soap and/or dilute the soap with water, 1 part soap to 1 part water before applying.
8. *Mold form box or clay wall burst while pouring plaster*	The form boards were loose, or the clay wall did not have enough reinforcement. Tighten the screws on the mold box; add extra coils to seal up the joins; add extra diagonal braces to the clay wall.
9. *Plaster did not separate from object or plaster section*	The original object or another section was insufficiently soaped. Try soaking the original and plaster sections in very hot water to loosen them. If the object was cast with an undercut, the plaster may not come out. With caution, saw the section that is stuck about ¾ deep into the mold on all sides except the inside. Turn the section on its back and, with a rubber mallet, whack the mold and snap it in half to break it into two pieces, separating it from the object.

Plaster Problem	*Probable Cause and Solution*
10. *New plaster poured on top of a section cast days earlier is cracking or drying too fast*	Moisture has evaporated from an old section, causing it to absorb water from the new mix. Resaturate the old plaster by soaking it for 5 to 10 minutes in water before pouring new plaster on top.
11. *Plaster mold sections do not line up after casting*	The object was moved during casting. *Or,* the object shrank or swelled during casting. An organic object like fruit will shrink, or a ball will swell due to heat generated from the plaster during the molding process, causing misalignment. Some objects need to be glued, weighted, or screwed down to a board before pouring. Vegetables and fruit should be cast all in one day, before they change shape. Wood, metal, hard plastic, or fired ceramic objects hold their shape during casting.

Slip-Casting Problem	*Probable Cause and Solution*
1. *Slip-cast wall is flabby and spongy, shape distorts easily*	The slip was undermixed or improperly weighed and blended. Always stir slip for a few minutes so that it becomes very fluid before pouring it into a mold. Mix a new batch of slip. *Or,* the mold was too wet. Dry it longer.
2. *Casting slip is too thick for pouring into a mold*	The slip was left uncovered and the water evaporated, causing the slip to thicken. Add a small amount of water. With caution, add a few drops of sodium silicate or Darvan #7. Test before adding to a full batch of slip.
3. *Slip gets clogged in the reservoir channel, or orifices leading to different parts of the mold become clogged*	The mold is too dry. Run the mold under water for a few seconds to dampen it. *Or,* the trapped air is blocking the slip flow. Add a few small cuts (1/16 in. [1 mm]) into the mold leading from the parts of the mold that do not fill, such as fingers on a hand.
4. *Slip is cracking in the mold*	The slip was improperly formulated. Mix a new batch. Resaturated dry scraps can cause cracking problems.
5. *Seam on slip casting is cracking; one side is thinner or thicker than the other side*	The plaster mold was cast with variations in the plaster-to-water ratio. Use a proper scale to weigh out water and plaster. Time the mixing so that each batch is mixed exactly the same way. If one side of the plaster was originally cast too thin, it will become saturated before the slip coagulates and forms a wall. Recast the section thicker, or add more plaster to the outside of the mold.
6. *Slip never dries in the mold, or there are spots on the interior of the mold where the slip constantly sticks*	The mold is too wet. Dry out the mold longer. *Or,* the mold is very old. Recast it. Slip sticking on the same spot could also be due to splashed plaster causing hard spots in the mold during casting. Recast the mold section, carefully pouring the plaster to prevent splashing.
7. *Slip-cast object does not come out of the mold*	Because they pick up soap and clay residue in the first couple castings, new molds may not cast well until the third or fourth cast. Try blowing a small amount of compressed air between the mold and the cast to dry and loosen the cast.
8. *Slip clogs on the inside of arms, branches, or other long, thin objects*	The drainage space for the slip is insufficient. Wet the mold with water before casting, and leave the slip in the mold for only a few minutes before draining. Insert a plastic rod down the center of a pour **sprue** leading up to the mold cavity to keep the slip from coagulating. With caution, add a few drops of water, sodium silicate, or Darvan #7 to thin the slip.
9. *Fired castings crack during bisquing or during third firing of china paint or luster*	Too much dried or damp scrap material added to fresh slip causes a chemical imbalance in the slip. Firing cracks often occur during the third firing. Do not add any scraps or trimmings to fresh slip.

4C

Preplanning for Installation

Preplanning is the secret when you must install work either temporarily or permanently. To eliminate later problems, think through the worst possible scenario and try to be prepared with all of the materials, tools, and helpers you will need.

LIGHT TO MEDIUM WORKS

For interior works, assemble installations on interior- or exterior-grade plywood panels before attaching the panels to the walls. It is popular for temporary or semipermanent installations. For outdoor installation, where water must not penetrate the wood; use high-grade exterior- or marine-grade plywood. For light pieces, sanded wood backing is adequate for surface bonding. For bonding heavier sections, score the wood and the ceramic sections to increase the gripping power of the adhesive. Inserting screws, nails, or bolts through clay sections and wood will ensure a safe bond.

Velcro is a trademark for a two-part nylon gripping tape that is used in ceramics primarily to adhere flat ceramic tiles to walls. Industrial-grade Velcro is best suited for use in ceramics because it has strong gripping ability yet comes apart easily. Glue one section of the tape to the ceramic, and apply the opposite gripping tape to the wall, using staples, glue, screws, or nails, depending on the type of wall. Press the two gripping tape sections together to attach the ceramic form to the wall.

LARGE WORKS

Preplanning before or while the clay work is in the damp stage prevents tiresome reworking and grinding later. Score damp surfaces that are to be glued after firing. Drill holes for screws or bolts in the leather-hard clay or greenware. Drill holes approximately 15–20% larger than final bolt size to allow for shrinkage in the kiln. Countersink holes so that after firing and assembling they can be plugged with colored epoxy, grout, adhesive, or mortar to hide the hardware. Sections may be mounted directly on the wall or attached to plywood panels and then mounted on the wall. Be sure that the plywood is dry and free of oil, grease, or other chemicals that could affect the adhesive. Be sure to determine whether that the wall construction will handle the weight.

CONNECTORS/NUTS AND BOLTS

Mild steel or plated steel is adequate for interior installation, but for outdoor installation use stainless steel, galvanized metal, brass, bronze, or other rust-resistant materials. Consult a structural engineer for information on which of these materials is appropriate for your application.

4D

Repair, Adhesives, and Adhesive Colorants

UNFIRED WORK

If a large section (more than ¼ inch [6.3 mm] thick) breaks off of an unfired piece, you can often repair it by wrapping the two pieces in saturated cotton rags, thus gradually dampening them, and then scoring and rebonding them with water or slip.

For smaller pieces, if you dampen the two areas with water, water and vinegar, or plain vinegar, you may be able to rescore and bond them again before firing.

For cracks, blend paper pulp with the same clay used to make the piece. Slightly dampen the crack with water, and then fill the crack. For larger cracks you can add fine grog to the paper pulp and clay. This will reduce shrinkage.

BISQUE REPAIR

There are commercial products that are advertised for repair of greenware and bisque were before refiring. Ericka Clark Shaw shares her formula for what she calls "bisque glue":

White glue	50%
Sodium silicate	50%

She says, *Add EPK (kaolin) and water until it becomes the consistency of mayonnaise* and apply. The glue can be fired to cone 10.

To repair broken bisque or greenware, sculptor Lourdan Kimbrell mixes a compound of 50% vinegar and 50% sugar-based syrup. Kimbrell says, *You can mix the vinegar with white glue, sugar, molasses, or any other type of sugar-based syrup. Blend the materials together into a paste, and add finely ground bisque clay from the same piece you are fixing, a little dry clay powder, and a ground-*

up pyrometric cone one cone lower than your firing temperature. The glue is best if you wait about one week, or until it smells like Camembert cheese. Then apply the glue to broken greenware or bisque, let it dry, and then fire to the appropriate cone.

ACRYLIC ADHESIVES AND MASTICS

These single-part adhesives for fixed works are appropriate for internal and external use to adhere ceramics to locations such as showers, kitchen floors, and exterior walls; to glue ceramic to ceramic; to bond ceramic sections with relatively flat surfaces with gluing gaps under ¼ in. (6.3 mm). They are also useful for gluing sculpture or light wall pieces, such as thin slabs installed indoors. Be sure to follow manufacturer's instructions.

EPOXY TILE-SETTING ADHESIVES

Also called *thin-set mortar*, these two-part adhesives consist of epoxy resin and a hardener that is blended with a cement/sand filler. They are usually gray or white. White epoxies can be tinted with glaze stains to match sculpture colors for repair and postfiring construction. They are especially resistant to physical abuse, salts, dilute acids, and/or cleaning agents. Epoxies bond ceramic to ceramic, ceramic to wood (interior only, unless protected from weather and with a properly prepared understructure), and ceramic to concrete, terrazo, vinyl, steel, stone, or gypsum board (interior only). **Epoxy should be used only with gloves and adequate ventilation to draw its fumes away from the worker and with a respirator rated by the National Institute for Occupational Safety and**

Health (NIOSH) for toxic fumes. Be sure to follow manufacturer's instructions.

For works to be installed in public places, consult a structural engineer before starting to build.

GLUING GLAZED SURFACES

For gluing glazed works to glazed surfaces, use silicon or epoxy for nonstructural, lightweight areas. For a larger work, outdoor work, or work coming in contact with moisture or water, before gluing it is essential to prepare the surface by grinding the glaze until the clay is visible. It is also strongly recommended that you make a physical bond using metal bolts or wooden dowels in conjunction with adhesive between parts.

A general-purpose polyurethane adhesive is adequate for gluing works to be placed in all extremes of temperature, moisture, and alternate freezing and thawing. These adhesives range in viscosity from thick pastes to pourable liquids. They have varying coefficients of expansion, which is important to consider when selecting an adhesive for gluing works for outdoor settings, especially under harsh weather conditions. Contact the glue manufacturer for technical information when using polyurethane adhesives in areas with adverse weather conditions or when safety in mounting a glued work is an issue.

PROPER SURFACE PREPARATION

Surface preparation is essential when gluing ceramic to ceramic or to other surfaces. Clean each surface thoroughly, and be sure that each is dry, dust free, and free of scale or loose parts. Painted surfaces should be sanded or wire-brushed until raw material is visible; metal surfaces such as steel, galvanized metal, aluminum, sheet brass, or bronze should be cleaned, sanded, or ground until shiny. Mild steel (non-plated or treated iron) is adequate for interior installation. For outside installation it must be painted, or use stainless steel, galvanized metal, aluminum, brass, bronze, or other rust-resistant materials.

COLOR ADDITIVES FOR EPOXY

The following coloring materials can be mixed with epoxy to color repaired areas or to glue sections. Because these colors are not fired, almost any powdered color, such as tempera or oil-base paint, will work. Universal oil-based tinting colors can also be used, and many intermediate colors can be mixed. The numbered stains are those available in the United States. Most stains available elsewhere will work as well but will not necessarily be tested for color results. **Since many of the ceramic stains and oxides contain materials that are toxic, they should be used with proper precautions. When using epoxy, wear neoprene gloves, have adequate ventilation to draw its fumes away, and wear a respirator rated by NIOSH for toxic fumes.**

The following table suggests mixtures of materials and colors useful for adding to epoxy when repairing ceramics.

Color Desired	Additive
Clear	Epoxy resin
Red-brown	Red iron oxide, concrete colors, Kreth red clay, Neuman red clay
Browns	Brown ceramic stain, concrete colors, burnt umber, raw umber, ball clay, Jordan clay, manganese dioxide, Barnard clay
Light brown/tan	EPK Kaolin, fire clay (Lincoln), cement, rutile
Light tan	Talc, white cement, dolomite
Black	Black ceramic stain (K470), lamp black, black iron oxide, cobalt oxide, concrete colors, black ink concentrate
Blue-green	Blue ceramic stain (#100 or 6254), turquoise blue stain (G490)
Blue	Dark blue ceramic stain (#1166), blue resin dye
Yellow	Yellow ceramic stain (F222A or #6433), cadmium yellow, yellow ochre, tin vanadium
Orange	Universal oil-based tint (yellow-orange), universal tint (raw sienna), orange enamel paint
White	Tin oxide, zinc oxide
Off-white	Talc, dolomite, Zircopax, Ultrox
Green	Victorian green ceramic stain (B211 or 1499B), chrome oxide
Pink	Pink ceramic stain (D320)
Red	Apple red ceramic stain (#6006), cadmium red (**highly toxic**), red enamel paint
Purple	Ceramic stains; mix pink and blue
Silver	Aluminum paint
Gold	Gold paint

5A

Sources of Health and Safety Information

NONPROFIT AND GOVERNMENT ORGANIZATIONS

The American Lung Association issues pamphlets explaining how to protect yourself against health hazards in the arts and crafts, with particular emphasis on dusts, fumes, and gases. Contact your local chapter.

The Art and Craft Materials Institute, Inc.
100 Boylston St., Suite 1050
Boston, MA 02116

The institute provides toxicological evaluation of art materials and compiles brand-name lists of art materials that are judged by the institute to be nontoxic. They also publish a newsletter, *Institute Items.*

Arts, Crafts and Theater Safety (ACTS)
181 Thompson Street, #23
New York, NY 10012-2586
(212) 777-0062 or 75054.2542@compuserve.com

ACTS provides information on ceramists' hazards and OSHA compliance.

ASTM Committee on Standards, American Society for Testing and Materials (ASTM)
1916 Race St.
Philadelphia, PA 19103

This organization sets standards for labeling hazardous art materials, which are revised automatically every five years and more often if needed. Write for a copy of the standards.

Ceramic Manufacturers Association
1100-H Brandywine Blvd.
P.O. Box 2188
Zanesville, OH 43702-2188

This association evaluates ceramic art materials in accordance with the American Society of Testing and Materials (ASTM).

The Cancer Information Service of the **National Cancer Institute** provides information on occupational hazards, as does the **American Heart Association.** Contact your local chapters for information on art hazards.

The National Institute for Occupational Safety and Health (NIOSH) is primarily concerned with safety in the workplace, but many of its standards also apply to ceramics studios. Local and state health departments, labor unions, and industrial relations organizations are sources of health and safety information, as are occupational health clinics, poison-control centers, and toxic-information centers at local hospitals.

State-run divisions of **Occupational Safety and Health Administration (OSHA)** are primarily concerned with safety in the workplace but are sources of information for studio standards.

State-regulated businesses, institutions, and organizations should contact their state OSHA for publications and compliance materials. Those under federal regulation should have a copy of the sections of the Code of Federal Regulations (CFR) that apply to their work. These are *29 CFR 1900–1910* (General Industry Standards) and *29 CFR 1926* (Construction Standards). Call your local OSHA office for information on obtaining copies of these codes.

Worker's Compensation Board of BC
6951 Westminster Highway
Richmond, BC V7C 1C6

Contact the Community Relations Department for a copy of *WHMIS Core Material: A Resource Manual for the Application and Implementation of WHMIS*. This manual is useful for all Canadian workplaces, but other OSHA regulations vary from province to province. Canadians must contact their local Department of Labour for copies of applicable rules.

In countries outside the United States and Canada, contact the appropriate agency for information on Health and Safety. Within the United States, state clean air agencies or municipalities may enforce ordinances that govern kiln emissions. In other countries, such as the United Kingdom, whose Inspectorate of Pollution requires registration for certain types of firing, you should contact the appropriate government office or local craft or ceramics organization for information.

Safety Equipment Companies (United States)

In your local telephone directory, you will find local and national safety equipment companies, many of which issue catalogues describing safety and health-protection equipment. These catalogues are often a source of information on respirators, gloves, dust collectors, supplied-air systems, ventilation systems, and other protective equipment. In addition, many of the catalogues of the ceramic equipment and supply companies listed in Chapter 5B include information on protective measures and equipment.

Direct Safety Company
7815 South 46th St.
Phoenix, AZ 85044

E. D. Bullard Co.
P.O. Box 187
White Oak Pike,
Cynthiana, KY 41031-0187
(800) 227-0423

Testing Laboratories (United States)

The following laboratories will test the glazes on your ware for the release of toxic material.

Bio-Technics Laboratories, Inc.
1133 Crenshaw Blvd.
Los Angeles, CA 90019

Coors Spectro-Chemical Laboratory
P.O. Box 500
Golden, CO 80401

Pittsburgh Testing Laboratory
850 Poplar St.
Pittsburgh, PA 15220

Twining Laboratories, Inc.
P.O. Box 1472
Fresno, CA 93716

5B

Sources of Equipment and Materials

GENERAL SUPPLIES

United States

Aardvark Clay and Supplies, 1400 E. Pomona St., Santa Ana, CA 92705

Aardvark Clay and Supplies, 6230 Greyhound Lane E., Las Vegas, NV 89122

Aftosa, 1034 Ohio Ave., Richmond, CA 94804

Alaska Clay Supply, Inc., P.O. Box 111155, Anchorage, AK 99511

Alpha Fired Arts, 4675 Aldona Lane, Sacramento, CA 95841

American Art Clay Co., Inc., 4717 West 16th St., Indianapolis, IN 46222

Amherst Potters Supply, 47 East St., Hadley, MA 01035

Annie's Mud Pie Shop, Ltd., 3130 Wasson, Cincinnati, OH 45209

A.R.T. Studio Clay Co., Inc., 9320 Michigan Ave., Sturtevant, WI 53177

Axner Pottery Supply, P.O. Box 621484, Oviedo, FL 32762

Bailey Pottery Equipment Corp., P.O. Box 1577, Kingston, NY 12402

Bennett's Pottery Supply, 431 Enterprise St., Ocoee, FL 34761

Bracker's Good Earth Clays, Inc. 1831 E. 1450 Rd. Lawrence, KS 66044

Brickyard Ceramics & Crafts, 4721 W. 16th St., Speedway, IN 46222

Ceramic Supply of New York and New Jersey, 7 Rte. 46 W., Lodi, NJ 07644

Ceramics and Crafts Supply Co., 490 5th St., San Francisco, CA 94107

Clay Art Center, 2636 Pioneer Way E., Tacoma, WA 98404

Clay Factory, Inc., 804 S. Dale Mabry Ave., Tampa, FL 33609

Claymaker, 1240 North 13th St., San Jose, CA 95112

Clay People, 112 Ohio Ave., Richmond, CA 94804

Columbus Clay Co., 1049 W. Fifth Ave., Columbus, OH 43212

Cone Ten Products, 6633 Pennsylvania Ave., St. Louis, MO 65111

Continental Clay Co., 1101 Stinson Blvd. N.E., Minneapolis, MN 55413

Corey Ceramic Supply, 87 Messina Drive, Braintree, MA 02184

Cornell Studio Supply, 8290 N. Dixie Drive, Dayton, OH 45414

Creative Ceramics, 5240 Aero Drive, Santa Rosa, CA 95403

Cutter Ceramics, Box 151, Waltham, MA 02154

Davens, 5076 Peachtree Rd., Atlanta, GA 30341

Dick Blick, 695 U.S. Hwy. 150, Galesburg, IL 61402

Del Val Potter's Supply Co., 1230 E. Mermaid Lane, Wyndmoor, PA 19038

Evans Ceramics Supply, 1518 S. Washington, Wichita, KS 67211

Felix Pottery, 1507 Hwy. 395, Suite A, Gardnerville, NV 89410

Freeform Clay, 1912 Cleveland Ave., National City, CA 91950

Georgies Ceramic and Clay Co., 756 N.E. Lombard, Portland, OR 97211

Great Lakes Clay & Supply Co., 120 S. Lincoln Ave., Carpentersville, IL 60110

Industrial Minerals (clay), 7268 Frasinetti Rd., Sacramento, CA 95828

Interstate Ceramics, 560 N. State, Oren, UT 84057

Jack D. Wolfe Co., 2130 Bergen St., Brooklyn, NY 11233

Jahn Ceramic Supply, 942 Pitner Ave., Evanston, IL 60202

Kickwheel Pottery Supply, 6477 Peachtree Industrial Blvd., Atlanta, GA 30360

Krueger Pottery, 8153 Big Bend St., St. Louis, MO 63119

Laguna Clay Co., 14400 Lomitas Ave., City of Industry, CA 91746

Leslie Ceramic Supply Co., Inc., 1212 San Pablo Ave., Berkeley, CA 94706

Marjon Ceramics, Inc., 3434 W. Earll Drive, Phoenix, AZ 85017

Miami Clay Co., 270 N.E. 183 St., Miami, FL 33179

Mile Hi Ceramics, 77 Lipan, Denver, CO 80223-1580

Minnesota Clay USA, Normandale Tech. Center, 6421 Cecilia Circle, Bloomington, MN 55439

NASCO, 4825 Stoddard Rd., Modesto, CA 95356

NASCO, 901 Jamesville Ave., Fort Atkinson, WI 53538

New Mexico Clay, 3300 Girard Blvd. N.E., Albuquerque, NM 87107

New Orleans Clay Supply, 3517 Chartres St., New Orleans, LA 70117

Ohio Ceramic Supply, P.O. Box 630, Kent, OH 44240

Priority Supply Co., 2127 Lake Lansing Rd., Lansing, MI 48912

Quyle Kilns (clay), 3353 E. Highway 4, Murphys, CA 95247-9604

Rovin Ceramics, 15333 Racho Rd., Taylor, MI 48180

School Specialty—Sax Arts & Crafts, P.O. Box 1017, Appleton, WI 54912

Seattle Pottery Supply, Inc., 35 South Hanford, Seattle, WA 98134

Sheffield Pottery, Inc., U.S. Rte. 7, Box 399, Sheffield, MA 01257

Southern Pottery Equipment & Supply (alligator clay), 2721 W. Perdue Ave., Baton Rouge, LA 70184

Standard Ceramic Supply Co., P.O. Box 4435, Pittsburgh, PA 15205

Trinity Ceramic Supply, Inc., 9016 Diplomacy Row, Dallas, TX 75247

West Coast Ceramic Supply, 756 N.E. Lombard, Portland, OR 97211

Australia

BPQ Controls, 14 Margaret St., Beachmere, Qld 4510

Hilldav Industries Pty. Ltd., 108 Oakes Rd., Old Toongabbie, NSW 2146

Keane Ceramics Pty Ltd., RMD 3971 Debenham Rd., Somersby, NSW 2250

Port-O-Kiln, 63 Dandenong St., Dandenong, Victoria 3175

Potters Equipment Pty Ltd., 13/42 New St., Ringwood, Victoria 3134

The Puggoon Kaolin Company and Ceramic Supplies, P.O. Box 89, Gulgong, NSW 2852

Venco Products, 29 Owen Rd., Kelmscott, WA 6111

Woodrow Industries Pty Ltd., 17 Kurra St., Lansvale NSW 2166

Canada

Ceramics Canada, 7056-D Farrell Rd., S.E., Calgary, Alberta T2H OT2

Culpepper, Box 36102, Calgary, Alberta T3E 7C6

Ferro Industrial Products Ltd., 345 Davis Rd., Oakville, Ontario, L6J 2X1

Hiro Distributors Ltd., 316 E. First Ave., Vancouver British Columbia V5T 1A9

Pottery Supply House, P.O. Box 192, 2070 Spears Rd., Oakville, Ontario

The Pottery Warehouse, 2071 S. Wellington Rd., RR #4, Nanaimo, British Columbia V9R 5X9

Saltspring Pottery, 13 Helen Ave., Kitchener, Ontario N2P 2E7

Tucker Pottery Supplies, 15 West Pearce St., Richmond Hill, Ontario, L4B 1H6

Tucker's Pottery Supplies Inc., 245 Griffith St., Stratford, Ontario, N5X 6T3

Woodlawn Pottery Supplies & Studio, 3784 Woodkilton Rd., Woodlawn, Ontario

France

AGIR Ceramique, Ferme de Regagnas 30770 Alzon

Ceradel Socor, 19 Rue Pierre Curie, 87025 Limoges Cedex

Ets Bermann, 7 rue Cartier Bresson, 93500 Pantin

Peter Lavem, 5 Rue de Picardie, 94100 Saint Naur

Poterie du Vieux Bac, 52 rue du Bac St-Maur 'La Croix Du Bac' 59181 Steenwerck

Sarl Multimat-Poterie, Eric Giverne, 46100 Cambes (Figeac)

Les Terres de Puisaye, 58310 Saint Armand en Puisaye, Les Perchers

Terres et Cendres du Berry Sarl, 'Les Chatelets' Neuilly-en-Sancerre 18250 Henrichemont

Germany

CREATION, Bahnofstr. 4, 56427 Siershahn

Kahlen-Keramik, Neuhausstr. 2–10, Aachen

Klück Keramik, Hafenwey 26, 4400 Münster

Holland

Keramikos, Prinses Beatrixplein 24, 2033 WH, Haarlem

Silex, De Meerheuvel 5, 5221 HA, 's-Hertogenbosch

United Kingdom

Acme Marls Ltd., Bournes Bank, Stoke-on-Trent ST6 3DW

W.G. Ball Ltd., Longton Mill, Anchor Rd., Longton, Stoke-on-Trent ST3 1JW

Bath Potters Supplies, 2 Dorset Close, East Tiverton, Bath BA2 3RF

Brick House Ceramic Supplies, Cock Green, Felstead, Essex CM6 3JE

C.H. Brannams Ltd., Roundswell Ind. Est. Barnstaple, Devon EX31 3NJ

Cromartie Kilns Ltd., Park Hall Rd., Longton, Stoke-on-Trent ST3 5AY

Fulham Pottery Ltd., 8-10 Ingate Place, London SW8 3NS

Hancock Pottery Engineers Ltd., Unit 4-6 Brookside Business Park, Cold Meece, Stone, Staffs ST15 ORZ

Kilns and Furnaces Ltd., Keele St., Tunstall, Stoke-on-Trent ST6 5AS

Laser Kilns Ltd., Unit C9, Angel Rd. Works, Advent Way, London N18 3AH

Northern Kilns, Pilling Pottery, School Lane, Pilling, Nr. Garstang, Lancashire PR3 6HB

Potclays Ltd., Brickkiln Lane, Etruria, Stoke-on-Trent ST4 7BP

The Potters Connection Ltd., Longton Mill, Anchor Rd., Longton, Stoke-on-Trent ST3 1JW

Potters' Mate, Cust Hall, Toppesfield, Nr. Halstead, Essex CO9 4EB

Potterycrafts Ltd., Campbell Road, Shelton, Stoke-on-Trent, Staffordshire ST4 4ET

Spencroft Ceramics Ltd., Spencroft Rd., Holditch Ind. Est., Newcastle, Staffs. ST5 9JB

BATS

M.C. Lueders Co. (hydrocal bats) 876 N. 30th St., Philadelphia, PA 19130

DECALS

Art Decal Corp., 1145 Loma Ave., Long Beach, CA 90804

Cerami Corner, Inc., 626 N. San Gabriel Ave., Azusa, CA 91702

TBR Decals, Inc., 824 Maxine St. N.E., Albuquerque, NM 87123

Wise Screenprint, Inc., 1015-C Valley St., Dayton, OH 45404

EXTRUDERS, SLAB ROLLERS

Bailey Pottery Equipment Corp., P.O. Box 1577, Kingston, NY 12402

Brent, American Art Clay Co., Inc., 4717 W. 16th St., Indianapolis, IN 46222

Northstar Equipment, Inc., P.O. Box 189, Cheney, WA 99004

Scott Creek Pottery, Inc., 2636 Pioneer Way E., Tacoma, WA 98404

FASTENERS

ThunderBolt and Nut Co., Inc., 2700 Rydin Rd., Unit G, Richmond, CA 94804

GLAZE

Amaco, American Art Clay Co., Inc., 4717 W. 16th St., Indianapolis, IN 46222

Ceramichrome, Inc., P.O. Box 327, Stanford, KY 40484

Duncan Enterprises, 5673 E. Shields Ave., Fresno, CA 93727

Great Lakes Clay & Supply Co., 120 S. Lincoln Ave., Carpentersville, IL 60110

Laguna Clay Co., 14400 Lomita Ave., City of Industry, CA 91746

Leslie Glazes, Leslie Ceramic Supply Co., Inc., 1212 San Pablo Ave., Berkeley, CA 94706

Mayco Colors, Inc., 4077 Weaver Ct. S., Hilliard, OH 43026

Sherry's Western Ceramics, 948 Washington St., San Carlos, CA 94070

Spectrum Glazes, P.O. Box 874, Lewiston, NY 14092

Unique Ceramic Colors, Drawer 20, Logansport, LA 71049

KILNS

AIM Kiln Manufacturing Co., 350 S.W. Wake Robin, Corvallis, OR 97333

Alpine Kilns, A.R.T. Studio Clay Co., Inc., 9320 Michigan Ave., Sturtevant, WI 53177

Ceramic Services, P.O. Box 1352, Chino Hills, CA 91709 (www.gaskilns.com)

ConeArt Kiln, Nidec-Shimpo America Corp., 1701 Glenlake Ave., Itasca, IL 60143

Contemporary Kiln, Inc., 24C Galli Drive, Novato, CA 94949

Cress Manufacturing Co., 4736 Convair Dr., Carson City, NV 89706

Duralite, Inc. (kiln elements, parts), 15 School St. P.O. Box 188, Riverton, CT 06065

Euclid Kiln, 1120 Speers Rd., Oakville, Ontario, L6L 2X4 Canada

Geil Kiln Co., 1601 West Rosecrans Ave., Gardena, CA 90249

Good Kilns, Sugar Creek Industries, Inc., P.O. Box 354, Linden, IN 47955

Jen-Ken Kilns, 3615 Ventura Dr. W., Lakeland, FL 33811

The Kiln Doctor, www.thekilndoctor.net

L & L Kiln Manufacturing, Inc., 6B Mt. Pleasant Dr., P.O. Box 2409, Aston, PA 19014

LE-Gas Kilns, Laguna Clay Co., 14400 Lomitas Ave., City of Industry, CA 91746

Olsen Kilns, 60520 Manzanita #205, Mountain Center, CA 92561

Olympic Kilns, 6301 Button Gwinnett Drive, Atlanta, GA 30340

Paragon Industries, Inc., 2011 South Town East Blvd., Mesquite, TX 75149-1122

Skutt Ceramic Products, 6441 S.E. Johnson Creek Blvd., Portland, OR 97206-9594

Steve Davis Kazegama Kilns, www.kazegama.com

Vcella Kilns, 171 Mace St., Unit B, Chula Vista, CA 92011

Ward Burner Systems, P.O. Box 1086, Dandridge, TN 37725

West Coast Kiln, P.O. Box 2152, Lucerne Valley, CA 92356

KILN SHELVES

Aardvark Clay and Supplies, 1400 E. Pomona St., Santa Ana, CA 92705

Cress Manufacturing Co., 4736 Convair Dr., Carson City, NV 89706

Highwater Clays, P.O. Box 18284 238 Clingman Ave., Asheville, NC 28814

R & M Supplies, Inc., 12011 Hueber Rd., Suite 210E, San Antonio, TX 78230

Smith-Sharpe Firebrick Supply, 117 27th Ave. S.E., Minneapolis, MN 55414

Thorley Refractories, Inc., 14400 Lomitas Ave., City of Industry, CA 91746

KILN VENTILATION SYSTEMS

Bailey Pottery Equipment Corp., P.O. Box 1577, Kingston, NY 12402

The Edward Orton Jr. Ceramics Foundation, 6991 Old 3C Highway, Westerville, OH 43081

Skutt Ceramic Products, 6441 S.E. Johnson Creek Blvd., Portland, OR 97206-9594

Vent-A-Kiln, 621 Hertel Ave., Buffalo, NY 14207

MOLDS

Duncan Enterprises, 5673 E. Shields Ave., Fresno, CA 93727

Pure and Simple Pottery Products, P.O. Box 337, Willits, CA 95490

POTTERY WHEELS

Axner Pottery Supply, P.O. Box 621484, Oviedo, FL 32762

Bailey Pottery Equipment Corp., P.O. Box 1577, Kingston, NY 12402

Brent, American Art Clay Co., Inc., 4717 W. 16th St., Indianapolis, IN 46222

CERACO International, 20685 Hansen Ave., Nuevo, CA 92567

Ceramic Services, 4780 Chino Ave. #B, Chino, CA 91710

Creative Industries, 1946 John Towers Ave., El Cajon, CA 92020

Great Lakes Clay & Supply, 120 S. Lincoln Ave., Carpentersville, IL 60110

Jepson Pottery Tool Co., P.O. Box 437, Geneva, FL 32732

Lockerbie Manufacturing, P.O. Box 2377, El Cerrito, CA 94530

Max Concepts, Inc., P.O. Box 7848, Colorado Springs, CO 80933

Nidec-Shimpo American Corp., 1701 Glenlake Ave., Itasca, IL 60143-1072

Pacifica, Laguna Clay Co., 14400 Lomitas Ave., City of Industry, CA 91746

Soldner, Bluebird Manufacturing, Inc., P.O. Box 2307, Fort Collins, CO 80522-2307

Thomas Stuart Wheels, P.O. Box 9699, Denver, CO 80209

PUG MILLS AND CLAY PROCESSING MACHINERY

Bluebird Manufacturing, Inc., P.O. Box 2307, Fort Collins, CO 80522-2307

CERACO, 20685 Hansen Ave., Nuevo, CA 92587

Laguna Clay Co., 14400 Lomitas Ave., City of Industry, CA 91746

Nidec-Shimpo American Corp., 1701 Glenlake Ave., Itasca, IL 60143-1072

Peter Pugger, 12501 Orr Springs Rd., Ukiah, CA 95482

Soldner Clay Mixers, 310 W. 4th, Newton, KS 67114

SOFTWARE

There are now a number of glaze-calculation programs available. Some of these are commercially available, others are free except for the cost of the disk and mailing. They vary in approach in what they cover, and in the ease of use. For reviews and up-to-date information on available programs it is best to turn to ceramics magazines or the Internet.

Annapolis Potter's Guild, P.O. Box 152, Arnold, MD 21012, USA

The Generator, Innovations and Frivolities, P.O. Box 431, Lancaster, NY 14086, USA

Glasure, Ulrik Krabbe, Ndr Strandvej 50, DK 3000 Helsingoer, Denmark

David Hewitt, 7 Fairfield Rd., Caerleon, Newport, Gwent NP6 1DQ, England

INSIGHT ceramic chemistry software: IMC 134 Upland Dr., Medicine Hat, Alberta T1A 3N7, Canada

UNIQUALC, J. B. May, 19 Church Rd., Boldmere, Sutton Coldfield, West Midlands B73 5RX, England

TOOLS

Brown Tool Co., P.O. Box 10758, White Bear Lake, MN 55110

Dolan Tools, 12612 N. 60th St., Scottsdale, AZ 85254

Kemper Tools, P.O. Box 696, Chino, CA 91710

Pierce Tools, Inc., 1610 Parkdale Dr., Grants Pass, OR 97527

Sculpture House, 100 Camp Meeting Ave., Skillman, NJ 08558

WARE CARTS

A.R.T. Studio Clay Co., Inc., 9320 Michigan Ave., Sturtevant, WI 53177

Bailey Pottery, Equipment Corp., P.O. Box 1577, Kingston, NY 12402

Brent, American Art Clay Co., Inc., 4717 W. 18th St., Indianapolis, IN 46222

Creative Industries, 1946 John Towers Ave., El Cajon, CA 92020

Debcor, 513 Taft Dr., South Holland, IL 60473

Laguna Clay Co., 14400 Lomitas Ave., City of Industry, CA 91746

Lockerbie Manufacturing Co., P.O. Box 2377, El Cerrito, CA 92223

Northstar Equipment, Inc., P.O. Box 189, Cheney, WA 99004

WEDGING TABLES

A.R.T. Studio Clay Co., Inc., 9320 Michigan Ave., Sturtevant, WI 53177

Debcor, 513 Taft Dr., South Holland, IL 60473

Lockerbie Manufacturing Co., P.O. Box 2377, El Cerrito, CA 92223